JAY G. LINDGREN

Therapeutic Group Work with Children

Therapeutic Group Work with Children

IS PUBLISHED WITH SUPPORT FROM THE

EDWARD F. WAITE PUBLICATION FUND

of the University of Minnesota Press

This fund was established in 1944 by George B. Leonard
of Minneapolis to honor the career of Edward F. Waite,
retired judge of the district court in Hennepin County,
Minnesota. Throughout a long life of service to the
community, Judge Waite has always shown, in word and
deed, an admirable social consciousness and a keen appreciation of the importance of friendship and understanding among peoples of all races everywhere.

THERAPEUTIC
GROUP WORK WITH
CHILDREN

Gisela Konopka

University of Minnesota

UNIVERSITY OF MINNESOTA PRESS, Minneapolis

LONDON · GEOFFREY CUMBERLEGE · OXFORD UNIVERSITY PRESS

FOREWORD

Mrs. Konopka's study of a group of delinquent children under observation by the Youth Conservation Commission is a most important one and is long past due. She describes in a clear manner the almost complete absence of a program of recreation and work in a setting which needs a very active program. The group of boys with whom she worked had been adjudicated delinquent and were waiting for a final decision of a group of examiners.

They were in the main an active, aggressive, restless group of youngsters. Added to this was the fact that they had committed offenses against society and so they were anxious, or guilty, or defiant. Without a program, the tensions in such a group readily mount to a high pitch with a resulting increase of feelings and reactions against society.

It is not surprising, therefore, that the introduction of a program of group therapy with these adolescents met with such hungry acceptance. The author's description of the details of the way in which the program was accepted, and how it was carried on, leaves little to be wanted. She is a forceful writer, has unusual powers of description, and indicates a quick perception of the emotional needs of youngsters. Her ability to change quickly from one type of activity to another when this is demanded must have increased her acceptance by this group of sensitive adolescents. The questions discussed with them during the discussion periods indicate the wealth of material readily obtainable in a program of group therapy when the therapist is skilled.

The experiment indicates the urgent need for the establishment on a permanent basis of Mrs. Konopka's demonstration program, as one part of a plan for therapy in an institution for delinquents. Such a program of group therapy must be supplemented by the provision of therapists who can work with individual children who do not respond sufficiently, or at all, to group therapy. In view of the fact that larger numbers of individuals can benefit from the kind of program that Mrs. Konopka has outlined, it would seem well to begin in this manner—and begin soon.

In the second section of her study Mrs. Konopka has described what took place in a group of girls whom she had under treatment a few years ago in a child guidance clinic. This study shows in greater detail the many situations which arise in group therapy, and the way in which they can be handled by a worker trained in social work and group therapy. Mrs. Konopka is presenting this material as an illustration of the therapy that can be done with children in the group setting.

Those of us who are doing direct treatment work with disturbed children in child guidance clinics, realize the difficulties involved in attempting to motivate the child to continue with treatment. We have recently instituted a department of group therapy in our clinic and already are seeing the greater benefits to be derived in some types of problems through treating children in groups.

In this book the material is recorded without an explanation of what took place in the relationships between the members of the groups to the leader and to each other. This was done intentionally so that the material would better lend itself to discussion in classroom teaching. Both sections of Mrs. Konopka's report should stimulate those who work with behavior disorders of children to add this approach to their treatment efforts. This implies a preparation in group therapy.

HYMAN S. LIPPMAN, M.D.
Director, Amherst H. Wilder Child Guidance Clinic, St. Paul, Minnesota

February 24, 1949

ACKNOWLEDGMENTS

In the summer of 1948 the University of Minnesota Graduate School gave me a research appointment to study the use of the group work method in an institution for emotionally disturbed and delinquent children. My special appreciation goes to Dean Theodore C. Blegen and the graduate school, who made the project possible.

The project was conducted in the reception center of the Minnesota Youth Conservation Commission, which is situated in the State Training School for Boys. Everyone involved gave help and encouragement to my work there. I would like to express my sincere thanks to Mr. Whittier Day, the chairman and director of the Youth Conservation Commission; to Miss Joe Ann Kramer, the reception center supervisor; to Mr. R. A. Farrell, the superintendent of the training school; and to the members of the Youth Conservation Commission, who allowed me to sit in on their meetings. My thanks go also to every member of the institution's staff who lent a helping hand, and last but not least, to the boys themselves, who helped to confirm my confidence in people.

This book consists mainly of records of group meetings. Since there are very few published records which describe group work in an institution, it is hoped that these will be an aid to group work study. In order to compare the results of this short-term experiment in an institution with a long-range program of group work with emotionally disturbed youngsters in an out-patient setting, some records of group meetings in a child guidance clinic are also presented. Little interpretation is given so that the material can be used in classroom teaching or in-service training.

I am indebted to the Pittsburgh Child Guidance Center, its board of directors, and its executive director, Dr. Harry M. Little, for permission to use these records and for the encouragement they gave me several years ago to start this group work project.

Finally, I want to express my thanks to my friend, Mrs. Anne F. Fenlason, professor of social work in the School of Social Work, University of Minnesota, without whose encouragement this book would not have been written.

GISELA KONOPKA

CONTENTS

To earn the right to belong he [the child] will adopt whatever code of behavior the gang or group prescribes, regardless of how much it conflicts with society's standards and demands. . . .

Give the . . . child this certainty that he belongs and is loved and you give him a chance to meet life with confidence and a willingness to cooperate.

JOHN R. ELLINGSTON in *Protecting*
Our Children from Criminal Careers

THE GROUP WORK METHOD

The group is a power, in either a negative or a positive sense, if we regard it from the point of view of society; but in either case it is a strong agent. "People solve most of their questions about living through their group associations." [1] How can we work with this power? How can we best use it to help our youngsters who have social difficulties?

There are many ways, but one way is to help them through their group associations. To every child, belonging to some group and having status with his contemporaries is essential. If this feeling of belonging cannot be found in a socially acceptable group, another one is chosen. The gang is often the only security that some youngsters know, and it is through this medium that they must find help. The child who is sent into an institution, torn away from his environment and his voluntary group association, needs additional help in finding some security and strength within himself, and also in adjusting to a new kind of group life. In such a setting it is the adult group worker's difficult task to make use of the interrelationships between the youngsters so as to encourage mutual acceptance and to help in guiding group mores and individual behavior toward levels that are socially more acceptable.

This, in general terms, is what group work consists of. As a method, it is based on an understanding of the group process and the dynamics of individual human behavior. It has been widely used in recreational and informal educational work with youths in our communities; but in addition to this, the method has been found to be helpful and even essential in therapeutic or correctional work with emotionally upset children and young people. The constellation of the group, the way relationships between members of the group are observed and used to help the individual, and the use of the individual's

[1] Bertha Reynolds, *Learning and Teaching in the Practice of Social Work* (New York, 1942), p. 89.

1

relationship to the group worker, an understanding and accepting adult—all these factors are not only essential in any kind of group work, but also are helpful additions to the process of clinical treatment.

Most experiments with the group work method for therapeutic purposes have been made with out-patient groups— that is, with groups composed of individuals who came to meetings at certain times and then left for home to join another group environment. Excerpts from the records of such a group are given at the end of this book. They are taken from a group experience with several emotionally disturbed adolescent girls at the Pittsburgh Child Guidance Center, and indicate how the group worker, as part of a clinical team, can help with diagnosis and treatment.[2]

The group work method has been used comparatively little in institutions for delinquent youngsters, though it is apparent that in those settings in which upset and emotionally disturbed youngsters live together constantly, the use of such a method by people who can handle it is essential. Several recent publications have pointed out this need and have complained about the lack of interest shown by group workers themselves. Susanne Schulze said in 1946, ". . . in the social group work field, scant interest has been shown in institutional work, in spite of the significance that this setting obviously has for group workers." [3] Paul Deutschberger pointed out that in work with delinquent youngsters we often separate them from the only security they have known, their gang, without giving them an opportunity to enter another close group association.[4]

It is interesting that the National Conference on Preven

---

[2] Descriptions of such experiments can be found in: Harry M. Little and Gisela Konopka, "Group Therapy in a Child Guidance Center," *American Journal of Orthopsychiatry*, XVII, No. 2 (April 1947); Fritz Redl, "Diagnostic Group Work," *Am. J. Orthopsychiat.*, XIV, No. 1 (January 1944); S. R. Slavson, *An Introduction to Group Therapy* (New York, 1943).

[3] Susanne Schulze, "Group Living and the Dependent Child," *Proceedings of the National Conference of Social Work* [1946] (New York, 1947), p. 387.

[4] Paul Deutschberger, "Case Work Failures and the Psychology of Restriction," *Probation*, April 1946.

tion and Control of Juvenile Delinquency called by Attorney
General Tom C. Clark in 1946, stressed, among other methods, the importance of the use of the group work method in
institutions dealing with juvenile delinquents. The experts
participating in this conference recognized how important
the group is to every youngster, and especially to the delinquent, who feels in conflict with the adult world. Often the
youngsters feel that "other delinquent girls are kinder and
more considerate than most adults." [5] The report of this conference summarizes:

All youth need experience through which their elemental desire
for friendship, recognition, adventure, and creative expression may
be realized. Juveniles living in institutions share these same interests with all youth. In addition, because they are temporarily separated from family and neighborhood groupings, they have increased need for informal relationships with others of their own
age as well as with understanding adults.[6]

Looking at our institutions, even the best ones, we know how
seldom they provide for "friendship, recognition, adventure,
and creative expression."

The National Conference reports summarize well the ways
in which the professional group worker can further the above-
mentioned goal:

(1) through an acceptance of the individual's feelings in his relations within the group; (2) through providing leadership sensitive
to the individual differences and needs of each member of the
group; (3) through the conscious use of group associations to
further individual development; and (4) through providing a
group setting in which individual recognition and group achievement may be used for socially desirable ends.

The problems of an individual requiring case-work services may
appear in his group associations as social immaturity, rebellion
against authority, inappropriate or exaggerated self-expression, hostility and aggression, timidity, and excessive isolation. During the

[5] National Conference on Prevention and Control of Juvenile Delinquency
(Washington, D.C., 1946), "Report on Juvenile Detention," p. 5.
[6] Ibid., "Report on Institutional Treatment of Delinquent Juveniles," p. 30.

past few years, group-work techniques have been developed that make "protected" or "special" group experiences possible for persons who do not fit into the usual or regular groups.[7]

The report concludes: "Group-work services should be provided for those apprehended for delinquent behavior, for those in institutions for detention, and for long-term treatment of juvenile delinquency." [8]

The group work method is based on respect for every human being, regardless not only of race, color, and creed, but also of age, sex, and emotional, mental, or physical handicaps. It is a method that refuses "doing for" other people, but hopes to help the individual and the group to learn to help themselves. This means that the group worker must know a great deal of psychology and psychiatry to be able to mobilize the forces which make this self-help possible. The worker also must understand the dynamics of sickness and the need to release hostility or anxiety before any positive work can be done. And, since he is working in a group, the group worker must understand the dynamics of group behavior: what a newcomer means in a group, what certain subgroupings mean to the individual. But most of all, the group worker must be comfortable in a group and able to handle a group. This is not the same as handling one individual or a sum of individuals. Every teacher knows that although Johnny may be easy to handle when one is alone with him, he can become a most unruly youngster when he is with two others.

The group worker has three main tools in his work. They are tools, never ends in themselves, because the goal is always to help the individual and the group to greater adjustment and better fulfillment. These three tools are the worker's own personality, the group relations, and an informal recreational program.

(1) To be really helpful to others anybody who works with people must learn to know himself, to recognize his own prejudices, his strengths and weaknesses. Intellectual book

[7] Ibid., p. 33.
[8] Ibid., "Report on Case Work-Group Work," p. 38.

knowledge of the dynamics of human behavior cannot replace a disciplined learning about oneself in relation to one's own work with human beings. I am more than ever convinced that a person working intensively with other human beings needs what we call in social work education "supervised field work"—not just practice, but a constant scrutiny of why we reacted the way we did toward a certain problem of our clients or group members, and why we did this or that in relation to a certain kind of behavior. Only a person who has gone through this process of learning will be free to accept love, hate, or resistance from the group members without becoming either conceited or discouraged or angry. The conscious use of his own personality is essential for the group worker.

(2) The group worker must understand group relations. He must be able to recognize the pattern of the group before him. He must try to answer such questions as: Who is the indigenous leader? Who is the isolate? Who make up the pairs, the triangles? Are these subgroups exclusive (clique-formation), or do they change?

Out of this picture grows the further question: What would be the most helpful grouping? As early as 1925 August Aichhorn said, "This matter of grouping is of first importance." [9] The group worker must not manipulate the group for his own purposes, but use the group constellation to help each individual in the best way possible.

(3) The group worker must know how to use program as a tool. For a long time group work was looked upon as consisting of program exclusively. Give the children something to do and they will be all right, was a frequent attitude. There is no question that activity is important, but by itself it will not help a child with serious problems. Many people have their pet recreations: "Baseball, that is it!" or "From now on everybody does fingerpainting, that is the therapeutic method!" or "Drama—let them play out their emotions, that will help!" The social group worker has learned that all these different

[9] August Aichhorn, Wayward Youth (Vienna, 1925; Toronto, 1935), p. 143.

activities are very helpful—music, drama, painting, ball games, handicraft, trips, etc. Without them he would work in a vacuum. He cannot help the individual in the group without these activities, but none of them alone and in itself presents the answer. They are only means to be used as an aid to help individuals with their interpersonal relationships. The better the worker knows program materials and when to use them, the better his work will be. Many groups are especially "difficult" and "upset" because of lack of skill and imagination in the use of program. On the other hand, however, program can be so overweighed that the individuals are forgotten and only the finished product or the winning of a game becomes important.

The group worker needs an informal, voluntary group climate to help the individual in his adjustment. While in many ways group work and teaching are very similar, this is the specific difference between the classroom setting and the setting in which the group worker functions. Even in an institution for delinquents, both attendance at specific group meetings and the choice of activities must be kept on a voluntary basis. Gordon Hamilton summarizes the importance of activities when she says, "There must be outlets for aggressive behavior in the children and the usual cycle of release, support, self-limitation by the group and ego-building through noncompetitive activities for the most part." [10]

[10] Gordon Hamilton, *Psychotherapy in Child Guidance* (New York, 1947), p. 169.

PART I. GROUP WORK IN AN INSTITUTION

The Setting of the Project

In the spring of 1947 the Minnesota Youth Conservation Commission came into existence. The new law provided that any delinquent youngster should first be committed to the Youth Conservation Commission for study and treatment. The Commission would then make plans with and for the youth, either for probation in his own home, placement in a foster home, or referral to one of the state training schools.

In April 1948 the Youth Commission was ready to open some of its reception centers, which were to accommodate the delinquent youngsters during this preliminary period of study and treatment. However, although the legislature had passed this law, it had not provided funds to establish independent centers of this type or to employ sufficient personnel. It was therefore necessary to set up the reception centers on the premises of the various state training schools and prisons, using their facilities and staffs. The boys committed to the reception centers were housed in separate units.

The training school for boys where our project was conducted lies in beautiful surroundings, and the reception center cottage is a comparatively new building. The number of boys committed to the reception center there had increased rapidly since April, and by August 1948, when the project was conducted, there were approximately seventy boys at the center. For this number neither room nor staff was adequate. Usually, only one man was on duty for this large number of boys, who ranged in age from eleven to twenty years. There were only

7

two small rooms and a large basement where the boys could spend their time during the day when they were not out-of-doors. Most of the time, because of the fear of escape, the boys were kept in the basement. This room was empty except for a long bench along the walls and the boys' open lockers at the other side. Recreational material available in the basement consisted of old magazines (comic books were not allowed), some files and plastic for boys who wanted to make rings out of this material, and playing cards. The attendant stayed in the basement with the boys, and the door was always locked.

A routine day at the center went like this: The boys got up at six o'clock, made their beds, and had breakfast. Meals were taken in the large dining room of the training school, but before the boys regularly committed to the training school came in, thus avoiding contact between the two groups. The boys always marched in formation from one building to another. After breakfast some of the boys helped with cleaning, while others returned to the basement. From about nine o'clock to eleven o'clock they did such chores as cleaning up the grounds, cutting beans for canning, etc. After eleven they were again in the basement for about half an hour to clean up for the noon meal. After the noon meal they stayed in the basement until one o'clock, when they marched to the library of the training school. The library is a very pleasant room with a great variety of books and some handicraft material. The boys chose their books and were allowed to take books out. During this hour they sat around tables and on the floor. At two o'clock the boys had gym, if no other work, such as canning, had to be done. From three o'clock to five o'clock the boys were either in the basement or outside on the playground, playing mostly ball games. At around five o'clock they had supper and after this they returned to the basement or played for about an hour out-of-doors before they went to bed. They slept in large locked dormitories. They were allowed to listen to the radio or read for about an hour after going to the dormitories.

This routine was sometimes interrupted by a visit from home for some of the boys, by a visit to the hospital for a check-up, or by conferences with the case worker, the probation officer, or the visiting psychiatrist. The boys never crossed the campus by themselves without a guard, except for a few boys who had the confidence of the staff and who could be recognized by their wearing of a special belt. Strict conformity was required. Punishment consisted mainly of "standing on line"—that is, the boy stands with crossed arms and is not allowed to sit down or speak or do anything else. Often the whole company had to stand on line if one of the boys had done something serious, like running away. Beatings were sometimes given as punishment, but this was definitely forbidden by the management of the training school and by the Youth Commission, and members of the staff were continually admonished to "keep hands off."

This quite drab routine was livened up by the human attitude of some of the staff members, and by the sincere efforts of the supervisor of the reception center to create a more therapeutic atmosphere. The lack of housing and the small number of staff members made a more flexible program quite difficult to achieve; but it would not have been impossible. The real reason for this stultifying routine lies in the basic philosophy on which our institutions rest. Unfortunately, our institutions for delinquents are still regarded as places where punishment must be given and where custodial care is all-important, rather than places of remedial treatment where the individual can be helped to gain confidence in our society, and in this way become a part of it. It must be said emphatically that the people in responsible positions did not adhere to the philosophy of punishment. They wanted a setup which would treat delinquents as the emotionally upset youngsters they are. They would have preferred a better program and a staff with love and understanding of children and with professional knowledge. They are constantly hampered by a lack of funds and by a lack of understanding on the part of the public. The responsibility lies not only with the policy-makers of our institutions, but mainly at the doorstep of every one of our citizens who wants these children "put away" without considering their need for real treatment.

This, then, was the background into which the project in group work was introduced. The group worker's role is that of a "change agent," as Ronald Lippitt aptly puts it; and in working with delinquents the change must be a change in each boy toward acceptance of himself and toward acceptance of social values. The dynamics of individual behavior are certainly different in every delinquent, as they are in every individual; yet almost all delinquent youngsters have in common an extreme insecurity, a lack of self-confidence (with consequent overcompensation through their delinquent acts), and a lack of confidence in adults and most other people.

Knowing that these were some of the general characteristics of the boys she would be working with, how was the group worker to begin? One of the principles of group work, and of all therapeutic and educational work, is to start where the group or the individual is. It meant, in this case, that some opportunity had to be given to the youngsters to release their stored-up hostility and to allow them some expression of their feelings. At the same time, this had to be achieved within the framework of the existing setup. Another factor that is basic to any attempt at therapeutic work is the formation of a good relationship between the worker and the person or group with whom he works. Group work uses the informal atmosphere of group meetings to achieve this relationship. Aichhorn expressed it very simply: "From the very beginning we felt . . . that above all we must see that the boys and girls from 14 to 18 had a good time. . . . they were human beings who had found life too hard." [11]

Gordon Hamilton indicates another all-important element: "The goal is . . . to release emotions without the accompanying guilt, to reinforce energies for insight and ego-building." [12] In the course of the experiment it became more

---

[11] August Aichhorn, *Wayward Youth*, p. 150.
[12] Gordon Hamilton, *Psychotherapy in Child Guidance*, p. 97.

and more evident that one of the most vital contributions the group worker in an institution can make is to create a situation for some hours of the day where the feeling of guilt is relieved, in this way freeing the youngster to come to more positive efforts.

With only one month in which to try out the use of the group work method, it was clear that no miracles could be accomplished. The following records are presented not because it is thought that they are perfect or free of all mistakes, but only to indicate what could be done in such a short period. The danger of subjectivity in records of this kind is also recognized, and whenever possible they should be supplemented by more objective tests, by verbatim recordings on a recording machine, and by intensive follow-up interviews. Such objective devices would add to the value of any conclusions drawn. Nevertheless, process records are rather reliable means of describing group work. They have been refined for years by social group workers and case workers, and have been tested for their validity during years of recording and supervision by skilled and practiced experts. Such records include not only what happened but also the group interaction, the verbal and non-verbal expressions as seen through the eyes of the worker who carries the responsibility for the group work process. The records in this book present only what the average group worker can contribute in an institutional setting. It is with humility toward the greatness of our task—the task of helping unhappy youngsters—that this work was undertaken and the results are published.

It was clear from the beginning that in order to give individual attention to the boys in the group, and to come to some diagnosis helpful to the Commission in making its decisions, the seventy youngsters at the center would have to be divided into smaller groups. It was agreed that the group worker should work with one of those smaller groups as continuously as possible. How to choose this segment was not clear, however. It was difficult to decide, since most of the youngsters were new to the center and since there was a fre-

quently changing population, new youngsters arriving almost
daily and others leaving every few weeks. The reception center
supervisor and the group worker agreed to leave the decision
as to which boys should belong to this special group until the
group worker had had some time to observe the whole group.
This was made possible by arriving on a Sunday, when all the
boys were playing outside rather informally, waiting for visitors to come.

Immediately following this introduction, a short case history is given of each boy who took part in the various group
meetings. These case histories were sent to the Youth Commission, usually by the welfare services of the home town or
home region of each boy. Some boys had had psychological
examinations at the training school, while others had not yet
had them when the project started. The case histories are presented in alphabetical order so that it should not be too hard
to turn back to the case history while reading about a new
name in the group records.

The records themselves follow immediately after the case
histories. The record of each meeting was written as soon as
the meeting was over. Excerpts from a group of records of
twenty-two meetings are presented first. These were the informal activity meetings, which were held in the morning
and in the afternoon, each time for two hours. In good weather
the group met in the garden behind the cottage, a lovely green
spot with benches and tables. Nearby was a large open place
for ball games, and in the distance beautiful hills could be
seen. On one side there was a view of a much-traveled high-
way on which trucks loaded with new cars continually passed.
When the weather was unfavorable, the group met in one of
the living rooms in the cottage. This room had chairs, a large
table, and rugs that could be rolled up. At times the group
was allowed to meet in the game room of the cottage, which
was equipped with a pool table, a ping-pong table, and a table
for handicrafts. Unfortunately, this room was not often available and there were restrictions regarding the use of the equip-
ment—for instance, the younger boys were not supposed to

use the pool table. The activities of the group were chosen according to the needs of the boys and consisted mainly of handicrafts, singing, and games.

The reader will find that at times new names appear in the records, or that sometimes a boy is no longer mentioned. In a reception center the population changes rather rapidly. Almost daily new boys were brought to the center by the police. On the other hand, when the Youth Commission had studied the case of a boy, usually some decision was made regarding his placement either at the training school or on probation. This meant that the boy left the reception center. The worker, therefore, could not always count on a stable group. In addition to this, the worker insisted on the voluntary aspect of participation in the group. When a boy did not feel like coming to a meeting for one reason or another, he was not forced to come. This accounts for some absences, though for very few of them. Other reasons for absence from the group meetings were visits to the hospital for a check-up or because of sickness, visits from relatives, or necessary individual interviews that could not be scheduled at another time. Only once did an attendant keep two boys away from the group to punish them. The importance of the group meetings as a remedial measure was explained to the attendant, and this did not occur again. This incident indicates once more the importance of staff teamwork in an institutional setting.

Following the records of the activity meetings, a group of discussion meetings is presented in which a smaller group of boys participated, and which represented a conscious effort to work on their problems after a relationship with the group worker had been established. Throughout all the records the names of the boys and attendants are disguised. The group worker is indicated by the initial "W." Evaluative and explanatory remarks, if necessary, are made at the end of some of the records; but in general the evaluation is left to the reader, since it is hoped that the records may serve as teaching material.

ARNE.   15 years.   Finished 7th grade.   IQ average

Arne comes from a family with average income. The family owns their own home, his father has work, and his mother is at home. The home is in a good neighborhood of a city and well-kept. Arne is the youngest of four children; two of the older ones are wage-earners.

Arne is unusually short for his age and looks more like an eleven-year-old than a fifteen-year-old. He has always had difficulties in school, has truanted often, and has had severe temper tantrums. When he stole a motorscooter he was first put on probation, then—after continued truancy—sent to the county training school. There he was classified as "incorrigible," since he refused any kind of work.

At the Youth Commission reception center he was referred to the visiting psychiatrist, and an electroencephalogram showed abnormal brain waves. He was given medication and it was impressed on him that he should continue taking this. Medication in conjunction with case work interviews and group work as described in the records helped Arne considerably.

(Arne was put on probation and went home at the end of W's stay at the reception center. Three months later he phoned to ask W to come to his confirmation. He said he now liked school and seemed to get along well. He showed his concern for others by asking whether the kids at the center would have something for Halloween.)

BILL.   13 years.   In 7th grade.   IQ 115

Bill is the second of two brothers. His older brother has been in the Air Corps and is now an airplane mechanic. Bill's father committed suicide when the boy was eleven years old.

Bill's very high-strung mother does day-work to support the family. Bill had been living with his mother in a well-kept three-room apartment in a small village. He had been a good student with no behavior problems, known somewhat as a dreamer and a rather quiet, solitary boy.

One day he burglarized a hardware store, stole guns, knives, and revolvers, stole his mother's bankbook, took several hundred dollars from her strongbox, hitched a ride, and stayed overnight in a hotel in a nearby town. He came home the next morning. When he was arrested, he brandished a gun and threatened the sheriff with it.

BOB.   13 years.   Finished 6th grade.   IQ average

Bob was born in a small town. His parents separated early, and from childhood on he was shuttled back and forth between different members of his family. He has an older sister. He has lived sometimes with his mother, sometimes with a grandmother, and sometimes with his father.

Bob has an early and long history of petty stealing, homosexual practice, and chain smoking. He was once sent to the county home for boys and after release from there was sent to a boarding home. There were continued incidents of stealing, and he was committed to the Youth Commission reception center.

CHARLES.   12 years.   In 6th grade.   IQ average

Charles is the youngest of seven siblings, of whom three no longer live with the family. Charles' parents were divorced and his mother had remarried, but the second husband had deserted the family. His mother was away from home most of the time because she worked. A grandmother who lived with them was often out begging in the neighborhood. The home was a sub-basement place in a run-down part of a larger city.

Charles was truanting, and had been shoplifting and stealing over a longer period. He was twice placed in foster homes, but ran away each time.

DALE.   13 years.   In 4th grade.   IQ 86

Dale's father is unknown. He grew up with his mother and his grandparents, who took care of him as well as they could. The family owned about forty acres of land, but their housing was very poor. Four people slept in one room.

Dale had been truant for one whole year. This seemed to be his major offense, although there was some indication of minor thefts.

FERD.   12 years.   Grade ?   IQ 89

Ferd is the youngest of four children, all the others being girls. Two of the girls are illegitimate. A few years earlier the children were found dirty and unkempt in a ramshackle house. The mother stayed away for weeks at a time. Ferd's father was an unskilled laborer.

The children, one of whom is feebleminded, became wards of the state. Ferd ran away from the children's home where he was placed. He did some petty stealing. He was placed in boarding homes and several institutions, but always ran away. He was then committed to the reception center.

GUS.   14 years.   In 7th grade.   IQ average or superior

Gus was picked up by the police more as a homeless boy than as a delinquent. He had been sleeping on roofs and did not seem to belong to anybody. It appeared that he had stolen a bicycle together with another boy, and it was found that he had run away from an out-of-state institution for homeless boys.

Gus was brought to the reception center mainly because there seemed no other way to handle his case immediately. Inquiries made by the Commission found his mother, who was anxiously waiting to find out where her son was. Gus is an illegitimate child, and had lived for a while with his mother, of whom he is very fond and who is very fond of him. She could not take care of the boy while she was working, however, and therefore had placed him in various institutions. Gus had difficulties in adjusting because of his fondness for his mother.

HARRY.   16 years.   Finished 7th grade.   IQ 90 or 115

Harry is an American Negro. His parents are divorced and both have remarried. His father is a college graduate; his mother was at home and worked part-time. Harry lived with his mother and four other siblings in a well-kept apartment. He was the second of the five children. He had difficulties in school and was said to be stubborn, but responded well to attention.

Harry did some stealing with a gang of boys, was put on probation, but was later found taking money from some drunken men. It was not quite clear whether he himself had done the stealing, or had been a lookout for the others.

HERB.   15 years.   In 8th grade.   IQ 95

Herb is the second of two siblings, his older sister being married and out of the home. Herb's parents are divorced, and he had been living with his mother and aunt in a comfortable home that they owned. Herb's father is remarried, and there seems to have been constant friction between the parents as to who should have the son.

At the age of thirteen Herb stole two cars, did some car prowling, and stole bicycles. He was put on probation. He broke probation one year later (a sex offense) and was committed to the county school. At this time the mother shielded the boy completely. After parole from the school he again broke parole by committing auto thefts and burglaries. He was then committed to the Youth Commission.

JOE.   13 years.   In 8th grade.   IQ 119

Joe is the second of three siblings. His father was a professional man, and was chronically drunk. During an absence from home he was killed, either in an accident or a drunken brawl. Joe's mother never told anyone about this, and the children think their father was killed in an auto accident.

Joe lived with his mother and a sister two years older than he in an attractive apartment in a house owned by his grandmother. He became involved in a long series of auto thefts. The first time, he was put on probation; the second time, he was sent to the county school for boys, then put on probation. After this he was again involved in car stealing and was sent to the reception center of the Youth Commission.

Joe had many fainting spells of an emotional origin. He had started psychiatric treatment just before his third commitment.

JOHN.   12 years.   Grade ?   IQ average

John lived with his mother and three older siblings in a rather good housing situation in a rural area. His parents were divorced rather recently and his father had remarried.

John showed great conflict over the divorce and did not know where his loyalty should lie. He also felt that his sisters were favored. He started to truant from school after the divorce of his parents. He was placed on probation on condition that he would attend school regularly. He failed to comply and was committed to the Youth Commission. It was agreed by everybody that he showed no other problems.

LARRY.   13 years.   Special class.   IQ 50

Larry is the youngest of three siblings. He lives with his mother in a well-kept but poor apartment in a fairly large city. Larry's father died several years ago. Larry's mother is very protective and fond of him, and has great ambitions for him

The boy was constantly pushed toward school achievement because his mother could not believe his mental inability.

Larry was involved in a series of minor thefts and finally in burglarizing a store.

LEO.   14 years.   Finished 8th grade.   IQ average

Leo is the third of five children. The two older boys are in the armed services, and one younger brother is in an institution for the deaf and dumb. The rest of the family lives in a well-kept cottage near a small town. The cottage is adequate in summer but too cold in winter. The family is constantly under severe economic strain, since the father is disabled and in a wheelchair, and the mother is crippled. They live on a too-small pension.

Leo had always done well in school and was known as a likable youngster. Fairly recently he started to steal cars. Since he could not drive well, he always smashed them up. He had been placed on probation but had continued his car stealing. He said he would be better off in an institution, since things at home were not pleasant.

LES.   13 years.   In 6th grade.   IQ 102 or more

Les is an American Indian, raised on a reservation. He is the third of nine children. Les has two physical handicaps, a cleft lip and only one arm. He had lost his left arm in an accident only a year earlier. In spite of these two handicaps he was not only an excellent student, but liked by everybody in the community and neighborhood. Reports on Les were outstanding in the praise accorded him by adults and youngsters alike.

Both of Les's parents were known as being constantly drunk. Les was afraid of his father and had shown, shortly before his commitment, a rather defeatist attitude: he had heard that drunkenness was inherited, so he believed that someday he would be a drunkard too. Les's older brother had also been in difficulties, but had been sent to an Indian school and was said to be very reliable.

It had seemed to Les that in order to get away from home and be allowed to go to school, he must get into trouble. He stole a case of beer with the help of some other boys and sold the bottles. As a consequence he was committed to the Youth Conservation Commission.

Lou.   13 years.   Special class.   IQ 51

Lou is the third of five children. He lived with his family in a six-room flat in a small town. His father was employed, but the family lived on a marginal income. The two older boys did some part-time work. The parents seemed to be considerate and affectionate toward their children.

Lou has a double handicap because of his low mentality and a hearing defect. He is an obese boy, small for his age, and strongly attached to his mother. The boy's offense is rather vague according to the records, but apparently he had been involved in some homosexual practice with older men.

Ned.   11 years.   Grade ?   IQ average

Ned is the fourth of five siblings. Ned's father was in the penitentiary for several years because of forgery. His father had escaped at one time and been hidden by Ned's mother, but he was then found in the home and taken back. The family lived in extremely poor and dirty housing. There was no running water and no indoor toilet. An older brother, a boy of superior intelligence, had been involved in sodomy and stealing.

Ned had always had poor school attendance and showed a history of continued stealing. While he was in the reception center his father was released from prison, established a better home, got work, and showed interest in the boy.

RALPH.   14 years.   In 4th grade.   IQ 88?

Ralph is the fourth of eight siblings. His family lives in the slum area of a small community in a tar-paper shack without running water or sewer. His father was for a long time on relief and now works as an unskilled laborer. One of Ralph's older brothers is in the state training school. The school and community for a long time rejected the children because of the bad reputation of the family.

Ralph was accused of several thefts, breaking into and entering a garage, and similar offenses. He admitted some, but decidedly disclaimed others, saying that his family was always accused of all misdeeds. At the reception center it was found that Ralph's hearing was greatly impaired, that he had diseased tonsils, a drooping eyelid, and bad teeth. He was badly in need of medical attention.

RAY.   14 years.   Grade ?   IQ average

Ray is the second of four children. While his parents were married the family constantly moved from one place to another. When Ray was seven years old, his parents were divorced and the mother kept the four children. Thereafter the mother worked and bought a home. Ray's father, who held a good position, remarried, and there were three children in this second marriage. He and his second wife and their family moved in with his first wife.

There follows a long history of the two families repeatedly breaking up, returning, etc. The oldest boy ran away. At one time Ray was sent to relatives for some months, but was called back. His life was a constant turmoil. Ray burglarized a school and was put on probation. A few months later he stole several cars and was committed to the Youth Commission.

ROGER.   14 years.   In 8th grade.   IQ average

Roger is the second of five children. He lives with his father, stepmother, and three half sisters in a new, comfortably furnished, attractive home, where he has his own room. Roger's father owns a small business and provides well for the family. Roger's older brother had been in difficulties and had spent some time in a training school, but was now employed.

Roger insisted that his stepmother hated him and that he did not like it at home. Nevertheless, his stepmother seemed to show real interest in him. Roger had been in difficulties since he was ten years old. At that time he was involved in several bicycle thefts and had run away from home several times. He was first on probation, then spent some time in the county school for boys. He then stole some cars and was committed to the Youth Commission.

Roy.   15 years.   In 8th grade.   IQ 67

Roy is the second adopted child of a well-to-do farm family. The family has a considerable amount of acreage and lives in a modern home. The couple who adopted the children had one son of their own. They are religious fanatics and belong to a strict religious sect which does not allow dancing, etc. The whole community has a very rigid attitude. The boy attended a church school, and it was always thought that he was "sly." There seemed to be little outlet for boyish needs. Since his "citizenship" was not good at school he was not allowed to participate in sports. Roy's parents showered him with gifts. There seemed to be strong sibling rivalry with his older sister, who was constantly held up to him as a model.

Roy did some stealing and was said to have fired a gun at his father and at a neighbor. Roy insisted that this was an accident. (It is W's opinion that Roy's low IQ may have something to do with his strong emotional repression.)

Ted.   13 years.   In 6th grade.   IQ average

Ted is the only son of his mother's first marriage. His parents were divorced and his mother has remarried. There are now three more children. The family had recently moved into a good residential area of a larger city. Aside from housing, the family situation was very hard on the boy. Ted's mother is feebleminded, alcoholic, and very cruel to all the children, and the father treats the children cruelly too. One of the children is an idiot, and the other two children are feebleminded and delinquent.

Ted was a truant, did some car prowling, and snatched a purse from a woman.

WALTER.   13 years.   In 6th grade.   IQ average

Walter is the fourth of seven siblings. Both parents work very hard and have a moderately well-kept home. Two years ago Walter did some petty stealing, finally breaking into a home and stealing some beer and pop, which some other boys sold. He was also difficult in school. He was placed in a foster home, but the foster parents soon felt they were too old to accept responsibility for the boy. He was placed on a farm, but soon ran away. He was then committed to the Youth Conservation Commission.

RECORDS OF ACTIVITY MEETINGS

Introduction to the Boys

W arrived at the reception center at around one-thirty in the afternoon. The boys, about sixty of them, were scattered over the playground waiting for visitors. The first Sunday of every month is visiting day.

Miss K., the supervisor and case worker of the reception center, introduced W first to ARNE. She told him that W would be around for the month of August and would probably take on a group of boys, but that W would like to know all the boys, if possible. Several boys sitting close by were interested and volunteered their names. One of them, RALPH, gave his name only when another boy nudged him. He seemed quite disgruntled. The supervisor also introduced W to BOB, who kept very close to W during the rest of the day. In order to become a little acquainted with each other, W and the boys kidded for a time about names and how hard they are to remember. More and more boys crowded around. They spontaneously told where they came from.

BOB very quickly attached himself to W and was apparently hungry for such contact. He said sadly that nobody would come to visit him. His parents are divorced and, as he put it, "I've been on my own since I was six months old." He said if somebody only cared for him he might not be here now, or "if they would let us little kids work." He is "in" for "armed robbery." W said that he did not look terribly tough, and he said he wished now he had not done it. He hoped he would get into a boarding home. He repeated twice, "Miss K. thinks this is not the place for me." He pointed several boys out to W, taking his task of introducing W very seriously.

RALPH was sitting on a bench, often staring into space as if he hardly saw anyone. Some of the boys teased him, saying that he told on others. RALPH said, "Nobody likes me here.

They say one of the boys was sent to the training school because I told on him." Bob said with feeling, "I like you, Ralph, and he would have been sent there anyway."

Some other boys came up to the bench. They asked what W would do, and if she would take her group off the grounds. They were obviously interested in anything new. A handsome boy named Ted joined and left the group several times. He was lively and seemed to be a link between the older and the younger boys.

There was some talk about the candy some of the boys were getting. They said that some of the boys would not want to share, but they would just take the candy away from them. There was frequent mention of the Commission, and how they wanted to get before it and find out what was going to happen to them.

Each boy also mentioned that three boys had "drifted" (run away) the previous day. They said that because of this the whole company (the cottage groups are called "companies") will have to "stand on line" all day for fifteen days (!) with their hands folded, and that they would not be allowed to play except on Sundays and when they worked. They said that one boy had wanted to sit down, but the attendant hit him. Mr. X., a housefather, is smarter, they said. When he had to leave the room he told the boys that they could sit down, because he knew that they would do it anyhow when they were alone.

W caught a ball thrown by one of the boys, and soon she and about six of the younger boys, along with one older boy of about seventeen, were engaged in a long and fast ball game. One of the boys, Ferd, was especially intent on making W lose. It was clear that he enjoyed trying to defeat an adult, but he was able to do it in an acceptable, almost friendly way. A young blond boy, Walter, sat around restlessly and dejectedly, saying sadly that nobody would come for him. W told him that it was only three o'clock and there was a good chance that they still might come, so why not join the game? He did so, and while they laughed and ran and caught the ball, he forgot the time and was happily surprised when his family finally arrived.

At around four o'clock the boys went inside. Two boys, Al and LEO, were on duty meeting the visitors. Both of them gave the impression of being especially friendly, sensitive boys. Al told W that he really is on probation, but that it might be a long time before they found a farm where he can stay. He would like to do farming. He said, "The hardest thing is to tell people that the time for a visit is up, but you have to do it." The other boy, LEO, asked W with great interest and intelligence what W was going to do at the reception center. He said it would be good to have somebody around who can make things a bit more pleasant—"Sometimes you don't know what to do." Then he added, "I saw you playing with the kids. You are the first adult I have seen playing with them."

W went downstairs to the basement where the boys spend about an hour before supper. It is a large empty room with benches along the walls. The older boys were together in one group, smoking and talking. Some of them sat in smaller groups playing cards. The younger boys sat around, doing nothing as far as W could see. Only RALPH was occupied, working on some handicraft.

W sat down between RALPH and HARRY, the only colored boy in the whole group. On the playground the boys had pointed HARRY out to W and had said that he can get "real mad." W had remarked that she wondered whether that didn't happen to everybody once in a while. BOB then told how he got mad at the county school and threw a billiard ball, and the other boys told how they got mad, too. Now W asked HARRY whether he had had visitors, and he said that he had and that he hoped to go home soon. He says everything in a solemn, hesitant manner. ARNE came over and was very affectionate with several of the boys, sitting on their laps and holding them.

The boys said that they were not allowed to have a movie this week because of the drifters. (The training school shows a movie every Saturday.) W wondered whether they might like to put on their own show sometime, and they seemed very enthusiastic. They wondered whether they could use the auditorium.

This time of day and the place seemed especially boring to the boys. We talked about other things to do, such as working with clay, and everything was taken up with enthusiasm. W had some pieces of paper and a pencil in her pocketbook and started some writing games. It was amazing what a hit these made. HARRY, BOB, TED, and RALPH played very intensely, and if W had had more paper many more would have played. BOB showed a considerable amount of intelligence and skill in the games. HARRY and TED were average, while RALPH was slow, but wanted badly to be in on it. When W began to tell stories and draw pictures, he became especially interested and tried to imitate her, much as a smaller child would do. The youngest boy in the group, NED, also joined in this group activity, but kept more by himself than some of the others.

While many of the boys were standing around there was again talk about hearings before the Commission. The date of the hearings, Friday the 13th, frightened BOB. Several mentioned their birthdays. LEO said, "A sad place to celebrate your birthday." (W felt that their birthdays should be celebrated somehow, since they meant such a lot to the boys.) There was more talk about W's group. Several of the boys— HARRY, BOB, RALPH, FERD, and an older boy—begged W to take them into the group. W said that we did not have to decide right away, and soon afterward the boys went to supper.

W met the boys after supper on the playground. All of the boys were outside—the older ones playing ball, the others doing nothing. A bunch of them greeted W right away and stood around ready to talk or to do something. It was obvious that they were waiting for some initiative from W. W asked who knew a good game. LEO, the same boy who had earlier spoken so intelligently about the need of doing something, suggested a running game, and about ten boys and W played this game with a lot of laughter until W was exhausted. W then taught them a new game that is played sitting down. Bob and Ralph showed again their great need for attention by their desire always to be "it." Interestingly enough, the other boys seemed very tolerant of this need. Before the play period ended several of the boys asked whether W would be around the next day.

Remarks

It was the younger boys, the thirteen- and fourteen-year-olds, who made the first contact with W and who seemed in greatest need of an accepting adult in this environment. They really are still children and feel rather lost.

The Sunday visiting day also creates a special need for a person who can give attention to the boys who have no visitors, and who can help keep going a pleasant group climate. Many of the boys are very upset on visiting days—for example, Walter and Bob.

First Meeting

In cooperation with the supervisor of the reception center, W selected a group of boys with whom she would work more intensively. Fourteen boys were selected as the nucleus of the group. They were chosen from the boys who had shown a spontaneous interest the previous day, and all of them were in the younger age range. Because of hospital appointments, however, some of the boys who were chosen were not able to attend the first meeting.

The boys who were to be in W's group were called. They followed willingly, while the boys who had not been chosen turned away reluctantly but immediately. They are very accustomed to the fact that they have no part in any such decisions.

Arne was practically dancing as the group went upstairs, so elated was he by the attention he had received. He clamored right away to sit beside W. The boys and W first sat around the table so that W could tell them what this was all about. W felt for the first time something like a group atmosphere, rather than a mass milling-around. Already in those few minutes, the boys had somehow become a group like any other group W had worked with outside an institution. They were still sitting neatly around the table—W knew that this would change—but the eager faces and the small number made for a different climate.

The attitudes of the boys in those beginning minutes were very different. ARNE was bubbling over, enthusiastic, and very responsive. HARRY was waiting, cautious, not very responsive. W had asked the boys to say their names so that she could learn them. W mentioned to HARRY that she knew some people at a settlement house he knew. He talked readily about this, but always with some caution. TED stared into space, looking rather helpless and bewildered. W mentioned a settlement house with which she knew he had been connected. He mumbled something. JOHN showed some hidden hostility by refusing to say his first name. He said rather angrily, "Since everybody calls me Baldwin [his last name], that is what my name is."

BILL seemed quiet—not very responsive, but not hostile. WALTER was almost as enthusiastic as ARNE, saying over and over again that they had had nothing to do and that he wanted to do so many things. LARRY said nothing and was almost immobile. LES seemed serious and very receptive, while CHARLES was quiet and looked rather distrustful. RAY from the beginning had something like a mocking attitude, as if he wanted to say, "This is all nonsense, isn't it?" NED was quiet, serious, and very much like the young child that he is, not quite fitting in with the others.

This is the picture the boys presented at the beginning of the first group meeting. Since they appeared in line, and since they were still conforming to institutional standards of behavior, no spontaneous grouping could as yet be observed. W started out by telling them that these were *their* group meetings, that she would bring materials and think of games, but that they, too, should make suggestions. W asked what they did when they were downstairs. "Nothing," they said in chorus. They wanted to do things and play games.

Before the meeting W had gathered paint, crayons, brushes, paper, charcoal, and paste. One of the housefathers had supplied a bushel basket full of gourds, which could be painted. W now distributed this material and let the boys choose gourds from the basket. This choice was one of the first decisions the boys made for themselves. ARNE showed imagination in the choice and use of his gourd, but because of his need for adult attention he often called for help. He said that he would make some salt and pepper shakers for W from the gourds. He also insisted on sitting beside W. LES, WALTER, and NED began drawing quite intently. Others took some paper but could not quite decide on what to do. Gradually CHARLES became very interested in the gourds—especially after he had been assured that he could take them home later—and worked out his own design. HARRY looked for pictures to copy. He is so tied up that it is impossible for him to do anything by himself, and he can only copy. He finally found a picture of a large dog and worked at copying this.

While the boys were working, some discussion was going on. ARNE started by saying that his home town was no place for children, and that there was nothing to do there. W wondered about the parks, but several of the boys complained that they always did the same thing at the parks—"You throw horseshoes and you throw horseshoes, you swim and swim." WALTER said that he would not get into trouble if he had a place to swim. Where he comes from there is nothing. CHARLES said that the county school was much nicer than here. There you could take long walks, but here you were always on the same spot. The others became quite hostile toward him, throwing at him the fact that he had run away from the county school. RAY, who was leafing through a magazine, said, "Oh, let him go," and the others stopped. This was the first time W saw RAY's power over the group, which later became even more apparent. The boys talked a lot of how they wanted to go up on the hill, just to see the country. This wish was repeated several times and was almost an obsession. The fact that going up the hill was not allowed seemed to them a further indication that they were not trusted. ARNE was very outspoken on this point, saying that they could be trusted.

While walking around the table W admired LES's design, which showed imagination, a real gift, and great anxiety. He had drawn mountains, a whirlpool, and the sun. The other boys remarked on the fact that he could do all this with one hand. LES smiled and said that he had learned to work with his left hand only a year ago. Several of the boys tried to write with their left hands. HARRY got recognition for his ability to write well with both hands.

The boys got restless and W suggested games. They played "Follow the Leader," and with the exception of RAY and HARRY all of them clamored to be "it." RAY and HARRY feel definitely older than the others, but are not free enough to express dislike of an activity. Instead, they just do not participate. Of the two, HARRY is the follower. LARRY joined in this game like a three-year-old. He enjoyed the clapping, etc., but when he was "it" he did not grasp at all what to do. He seemed completely frustrated when in this position and held his hands before his eyes, a gesture he always repeated when he felt frustrated. The other boys seemed quite tolerant of him at this point. JOHN was on the periphery most of the time, occasionally wrestling with TED. NED became more animated during the games.

W then suggested—the boys themselves made no suggestions—that each one act out what he wanted to be when he was twenty years old. This was done in pantomime and the others had to guess. Their choices were: ARNE: a trainman; HARRY: unable to express anything; NED: dogcatcher—performed with great gusto; TED: could not do it; CHARLES: shoemaker—but he said later that he did not really mean it; JOHN: traveling salesman; RAY: food sampler; BILL: painter; LES: artist-painter; WALTER: [W forgets].

ARNE mentioned that he would be married when he was twenty. Since the boys wanted more of this activity they proposed acting out what they would do when they were

married. It seemed to W that it was typical of a first meeting
that the resulting scenes were so conventional. In one skit
RAY was the wife who washed dishes—this produced a big
laugh—and WALTER handed his paycheck over to her. In another, ARNE was the wife and played dreamily on the piano
while NED, as the husband, listened.

It was then time to leave.

Second Meeting

The boys were waiting downstairs at the steps, and W
heard them shout, "There she is." Already in this second
meeting they relaxed, were more at ease, and were much less
conforming. This meant that work with them would be harder
and that resistances would now appear. BOB, RALPH, LEO,
and FERD were present for the first time. Since all four of them
had already had quite a lot of contact with W, they quickly
became part of the group. All four are quiet boys. BOB watches
W with eyes that hang on every movement. The boy is starved
for affection and reaches out for it. LEO was more quiet than
previously and very helpful in activities. RALPH needs a great
deal of attention. He has a hard time in the group, is apparently not well accepted, and is often teased. FERD was rather
quiet, but seemed easily provoked by the other boys.

The boys started with painting, which was much more attractive to them than drawing. RAY showed more and more
his superior attitude toward everything offered. He drew some
very good figures, but invariably he would destroy them and
paint something nondescript. Once, when he painted a lot
of blue nothing, there appeared for the first time a sign of
group control. The boys sitting beside him (W thinks they
were ARNE, JOHN, and WALTER) objected to his "wasting
paint," and he really stopped. He frequently made loud and
rather cruel remarks, which the others apparently took from
him without objection, although they would have resented
them coming from anyone else. He said, for instance, that he
would trust everyone in the group except HARRY (the only
Negro), and after a pause he added, "HARRY can hide in the

dark." HARRY did not object. When W protested, RAY said that he was HARRY's pal and therefore could say what he had. HARRY confirmed this. Later RAY said that LES had something special—he had only one arm. Like HARRY, LES did not object.

The boys drew for a while, then spontaneously reached out for different games. Small subgroups built and fell, apparently following an age pattern, with RAY, HARRY, and JOHN as the oldest group, rather aloof from the others. Throughout the whole afternoon CHARLES sat quietly by himself, intent on painting.

When the boys became restless with the games, W started them singing. ARNE and BOB sang very well, carrying the tune. W encouraged TED to sit close by. He seemed to enjoy this, though he did not sing. HARRY took full part in the singing and seemed to enjoy it at this point. The boys shared songbooks quite well.

RAY started some stunts, and the group, readily following him as always, again became restless. W suggested a "show" and became the announcer. They seemed to enjoy W's announcing their names prefixed by "Mr." and her appreciation of their humor. ARNE sang seriously a funny song. TED, who usually was somewhat on the periphery of the group, became more lively and stood on his head. After this it was headstands for almost all of them, with WALTER trying to pull the carpet out from under them to make them fall.

Remarks

The change in climate from the usual atmosphere of the reception center was outstanding. During these meetings the boys seem to be relieved of some pressure; they relax and become more themselves. The more this release from guilt is felt by the boys, the harder they will be to handle.

At this meeting RAY showed himself to be something of a natural gang leader—attractive, physically strong, less afraid of adult authority than most of the others, admired by the others but quite cold toward them.

The program at this meeting consisted almost entirely of various activities, with verbal expression only at an informal level.

Third Meeting

. . . Bob said that he wanted to paint, but did not know how. He looked quite depressed and was extremely quiet. W encouraged him to use charcoal and to express whatever he was thinking about. He drew some mountains with deep shadows and wrote in each corner of the picture a name, one girl's name and three boys' names. W asked him who they were. He said they were his sister and three other boys. "All people you like?" "All I have," he said, "and it is sad." Later, he again drew two mountains and an American flag between them, saying that this was not so sad. He was by himself most of the time during the meeting.

Fourth Meeting

The boys were watching a ball game, and W said that she did not want to interfere but would watch along with them. Arne objected strongly, saying, "This is our time." Since most of the younger boys also preferred to have the group meeting, they all left the ball game.

Walter and Ralph suggested a running game, but somehow it was very hard to get the boys together. Only Walter, Ted, Charles, and Arne played, while the others drifted around, sometimes joining in, sometimes talking at the water fountain. Ferd seemed to be everywhere he shouldn't be and started squirting water around. W called the boys together and asked them what they really wanted to do. Nobody had *told* them to play running games; did they want to or not? There was a loud clamor for volleyball and almost as much objection. W asked for a show of hands for volleyball, and found to her surprise that the "loud clamor" had come from only four boys, Charles, Ted, Walter, and a fourth whom W forgets. All the others preferred painting. Ted said angrily, "Oh, that means no volleyball." W asked why he thought so;

couldn't we divide the group? W asked him to bring the volleyball, and for the rest of the afternoon those four played very happily, while the others formed a group far more harmonious than they had been in the morning.

At this meeting HARRY was more a part of the group, though he still was unable to do anything very definite. Lou did a little painting but in general looked rather forlorn. Lou had arrived at the center the previous day. He had been terribly afraid about coming there, and when on his arrival he heard the group singing he had almost cried with relief. The friendly probation officer who brought him had pleaded that Lou be allowed to join the group, and W had agreed. Lou gave the impression of being quite a dull boy, unable to compete with the others and frequently teased because of his obesity. NED and LEO were very intent on painting. W sat across from LEO, and he told her that he had talked to Miss K. He said he wished he had not done what he had. He had stolen some cars, but he looked as if he could hardly realize the fact.

Some of the other boys joined the conversation. HARRY said how much he disliked school. JOHN said that he was here only because he had quit school. He had promised the judge to take two subjects in summer school, but he had taken only one. He did not think that was so terrible. RALPH said he had quit school and would not go back. W wondered what was so especially disagreeable about school. "The teachers," and, "It's boring," were the answers. NED, however, said that he wanted to go back to school and stay in school. He was practically hooted down. He stood his ground halfway, saying that he was not very fond of school, but that he wanted to finish it. (This was an interesting example of group pressure in an undesirable direction.) W gave NED encouragement by nodding, but not too many words, since the latter would have increased the resentment of the others toward him.

Fifth Meeting

Before the meeting, Miss K., the supervisor, told W of some very interesting comments she had received from two of the boys regarding the meetings. Leo had come to her asking whether she could not tell the boys to be more disci-plined when they were with W. He felt the boys were rude to W. Miss K. told him that W did not want the boys to be restricted in this way. She said that W would handle the problem when necessary, but that both she and W felt the boys should learn to get along when they were not told what to do all the time. Leo was somewhat reassured, but continued to show concern.

Arne had also come to Miss K., saying that he did not want to be in the group, that it was "baby stuff." She replied that that was all right, that this was a group where the boys had a right to choose, and that he did not need to go. He should just tell W and he would be taken off the list. Arne then said that he did not want to hurt W's feelings. Miss K. said that he would not, and that he could say what he thought. This pulled the last "projection" from under his feet, and he said that he did not see why he should have this right to choose, when otherwise he was never allowed to say what he wanted. Why did she want him to say that he wanted to get out of the group? Miss K. replied that she did not want him to say that, but it was good to have something to say. Arne then asked how he had got into the group. Miss K. explained how she and W had observed the boys and thought this group would fit together. He angrily asked her why she wanted him to leave the group when it was the one thing he really liked here? She said she seemed to be all mixed up. Hadn't he said he wanted to leave? He said, "You are mixed up about a lot of things," and then began to tell her how glad he was that he could talk to her.

(This episode showed how helpful it can be for case worker and group worker to work together on such a project. Team-work of this kind necessarily requires maturity and professional attitudes on both sides, since both workers must be able to take criticism and to understand the psychological mechanisms involved. It seems very important for the boys to have two people with whom they can establish relations of trust and with whom they can be frank. It is also important that all the adults concerned show consistency in their approach to the youngsters.)

At the fifth meeting W brought a pail of water and some clay powder. When the boys came out to the meeting TED, ARNE, and RALPH started to mix the clay. Of the three, RALPH was the one who knew best what to do and gave instructions. Only about six of the boys did clay work, but those who chose it worked very intently. The others continued their painting. RAY was far more positive at this meeting. He used his sense of humor and leadership ability in a more constructive way. He made a head with a funny face out of the clay and enjoyed finishing it.

This was a satisfied, well-occupied group, with the exception of LARRY. He continually stood isolated, without moving. When spoken to he would answer, but there was no positive response. (W's suspicion of psychosis in LARRY's case was growing.)

Some older boys not in the group started to play volleyball nearby, and RAY asked to join them. W gave her permission. He showed a special interest in games of this kind and was accepted by the older boys. W had the impression that this permission meant something to the others too. They realized that they really could make a choice. BILL played a lot with the clay and threw it around, but finally settled down and helped BOB make an ashtray. It was the first time that W observed two of the boys really working together and doing so spontaneously. Together they did a very good job. While the boys were working there was some talk about smoking. (Boys under sixteen are not allowed to smoke at the center. The older boys form a line three times a day and receive some smoking material.) All the boys, with the exception of NED, said they smoked, and they discussed their preferences for certain brands.

LEO wondered whether there should not be more discipline in the group. Since W knew from the supervisor that he was concerned about this, she went into the subject a little more deeply. She asked whether there was anybody who would tell them what they should do and not do when they got out of here. LEO said that there certainly was not. W explained then that it seemed a good idea for them to have one place here where they could learn to make some of their own decisions. W caught ARNE's look and saw that he was listening intently. He was apparently somewhat upset by this discussion, and interrupting the talk, asked W to draw a boat for him. She did, and he soon started making a boat out of clay.

Sixth Meeting

W asked whether the boys wanted to play games. No, they much preferred to do painting. CHARLES especially was very intent on it. While he was working he said how much he loved it, and that he had done similar things at the YMCA. CHARLES was beginning to talk more than in the first meetings, and worked very absorbedly on all handicraft. He and NED were together a great deal and had similar interests.

ARNE continued working on his clay boat, which W had kept moist for him. W thought he had done an exceptionally smooth job on it and said so. ARNE replied angrily that W seemed to like everything, but he did not think it was good at all. He seemed so little used to acceptance that he almost resented it. W said she really thought it was good, otherwise she would not say so. He asked W in the same angry tone of voice why she bought clay in powder form instead of ready-made clay. W explained that the powdered clay was less expensive. "So what," he said, "I don't pay for it." W said she knew that, but it was public money that went into all this and so we could not waste it. LEO joined in, saying that everything else costs money too. ARNE said he didn't care, he wasn't a taxpayer. LEO and BOB objected to this attitude and told ARNE not to say such things before W. W said she preferred people to speak their minds while she was present rather than behind her back. ARNE, less defiantly, said, "Well, I do, don't I?" W smiled and said he certainly did. In one of his quick changes of mood he smiled too, and the conversation shifted.

It was interesting that after this ARNE returned to work very carefully on his boat.

Seventh Meeting

. . . BILL and LES were sitting quietly on the ground talking when W joined them for a little while. LES said that what they were talking about was not pleasant, since he was telling BILL about the Indian reservation. He said he did not mind the reservation as such, but that there was not enough work and people hadn't enough to live on. Then "white man," as LES says, would always come and trade them alcohol for meat, and there was too much drinking. His father had had enough money when he came home from the navy, and they had lived well when he had been in the service; but then he started drinking and he had to sell his horse and his cow.

RALPH had joined the group now, and he said that his uncle went trading at the reservation. LES said his family had too many children—there had been nine of them. RALPH said that they had been nine children too, but this was nothing. A friend of his mother had always said she never wanted a family, and now she had sixteen children and kept them all cooped up in the garage. LES shook his head and said that the white man always thinks he is better than the Indian. W asked if his people were allowed to go off the reservation. He said they were, but that sometimes they don't find work because they have not learned anything, and it takes so long and meanwhile their families have nothing to eat. He said, "When they get too much from the welfare, they take the children away." W asked him about school. He said it was okay, but that he had never seen an Indian who had been to college. LES said these things matter-of-factly, not in a complaining way but in great earnest. Throughout the discussion BILL listened with compassion.

Eighth Meeting

The boys had clamored continuously to stay in and play pool and ping-pong. In the morning LEO had said that he was praying for rain. Since it was cloudy, W suggested that they go into the game room. A wild storm of enthusiasm greeted this suggestion, and the boys ran to the pool table, ARNE showing more aggression than the rest. W had a hard time creating any order out of the chaos, but finally suggested that she would choose four boys to start playing. In ten minutes they would change off and another four take their places. This proposal met with general acceptance, but also with considerable howling from all sides that each one wanted to be first. LEO, RAY, and HARRY were the first ones to say that they would just as soon play later, and then a number of the others followed their example. WALTER, TED, and ARNE were most insistent on being first.

While the first four boys played pool, the others did some felt work. W had brought pieces of brightly colored felt, large needles, and yarn, and the boys enjoyed making pocketbooks and purses and cutting out letters. W had started the sewing for several of them, and WALTER, after his turn at the pool table was up, became the image of a happy little boy when he found that W had started his work. He was especially happy that W had done "something for him," and he became engrossed and learned to sew very quickly. NED and CHARLES said they knew how to sew and did, although NED had a rather hard time at it. CHARLES talked about the county school. One of the physical education instructors had come to the reception center to visit, and CHARLES said that he had known him there and also earlier at the YMCA.

The room was filled with a great deal of noise and it was sometimes hard to hear each other. Whenever a turn at the pool table was up, there were some complaints about not having had enough time, but after about an hour not quite so many wanted to play and things calmed down somewhat. JOHN complained about feeling sick, but DALE went downstairs with him, and he soon felt better. This was DALE's first time with the group. He had been on duty at the hospital, waiting for placement. He had stolen some mercury from the hospital and therefore had been sent back to his company. Because of this failure, some special help for DALE was indicated, and W's group was the only help available.

At one point there was a scuffle around the pool table. W had assigned RALPH to play, not realizing that it was not yet his turn. RAY had pushed him, and RALPH sat on a chair, crying and doubled up as if in agony. RAY said that RALPH was a crybaby. W said he might be really hurt and asked what was it all about. After the boys explained, W said to RAY that it was really her fault, wasn't it, and next time he should hit W and not the other boy. RAY's face looked blank, then he smiled—for the first time, W thought, warmly, without his usual irony—and said twice, "I'm sorry, RALPH." W asked RALPH if he felt really bad, but he shook his head. After he had finished crying he came up to the table and seemed to feel better.

RAY clamored for the election. (This election of officers for the group had been proposed on an earlier occasion.) W agreed that they could at least start it and go on tomorrow. She asked RAY to write down the different offices, and he did, asking frequently about the spelling. W tried to call the boys together and calm them, but it seemed an impossible task. RAY again became the leader, in the rough manner of the gang boss who knows how to handle them. He pulled the boys around and pushed little NED into the circle. NED hit back, and there was some minor scuffling. ARNE sulked in a corner, saying that he did not want any office anyway. RAY suggested the following officers: one mayor, one judge, two policemen, three from the jury, one probation officer, and one sheriff—a list of "government" officials that certainly seemed indicative.

W asked who wanted to run for mayor, and RAY and CHARLES volunteered. When speeches were demanded, RAY became tongue-tied and murmured something about giving good government and sending the kids to the judges and probation officer. CHARLES was less embarrassed. He said that he would run the city well. For judge, WALTER and BOB volunteered. WALTER said he would talk to the kids and make them listen. BOB's short speech, in which he promised real justice, was the most grown-up of the group. DALE and NED volunteered for the police. DALE said in his friendly, warm manner that he would bring the kids into court and would not hurt them. NED said he would do the same and watch them. TED had waited impatiently to say that he wanted to be a probation officer. He said that that was something he really wanted to be someday. (Earlier in the meeting his probation officer had dropped in.) RALPH wanted to be one too. In his campaign speech TED said, "Well, you know how things are nowadays. The kids get into trouble." He said he would talk to the kids and try to keep them out of trouble. RALPH repeated this somewhat. ARNE, who had said he was not interested in an office, jumped up and clamored to be made sheriff. Nobody else asked for it. He said he would be strict and make the kids do what they were told. One of the boys asked W anxiously whether this would really be true. The campaign speeches ended the meeting, with the election scheduled for the following day.

Ninth Meeting

Before the meeting W had typed ballots for the election, according to the wishes of the boys. Since W felt that these ballots would be a great help in measuring group acceptance, she added a write-in blank for sheriff, an office for which only ARNE had volunteered. For W's own purposes of observation she also added: "Name who would be the best leader of the group." The ballots were distributed and pencils were ready when the boys came. They were interested in this procedure and took the voting seriously. LARRY could not read and was helped by TED. LOU could not read either, and W, after starting to help him, asked RALPH to continue helping him, which he did.

After the election some of the boys started playing ping-pong, others reached for the felt work, and still others wanted to play pool. BOB, under the close supervision of JOHN, TED, and Bill, started to count the ballots. The results of the voting were:

Office	Name	No. of Votes
Mayor	Charles	3
	Ray	13
Judge	Walter	14
	Bob	5
Policeman	Dale	11
	Ned	5
Probation Officer	Ted	10
	Ralph	4
Sheriff	Arne	4
	Bill	4
	Harry	3
	Dale	3
	John	1
Best Leader	Dale	3
	Ralph	1
	Ted	2
	Harry	7

Discrepancies in the number of votes were the result of not every boy voting on every office. Leo and Les did not take part in the elections, Leo because he had become a messenger for the office and no longer attended the group regularly, and Les because he had to take a test that day. It is interesting that although Arne's name was the only one listed on the ballot for sheriff, so that the boys had to write in a name if they did not want him, only three boys voted for him, the fourth vote being his own. When a vote was taken to decide the tie between him and Bill, Bill won.

There are other significant facts to learn from this election. Every boy who had his name on the ballot voted for himself, yet none of the boys used his own name as a write-in or voted for himself as the best leader. Both these facts show a considerable amount of group spirit.

Chart 1 shows the way preferences expressed themselves

Chart 1. Group Relations as Expressed in the Choice of the Best
Leader at the Ninth Meeting

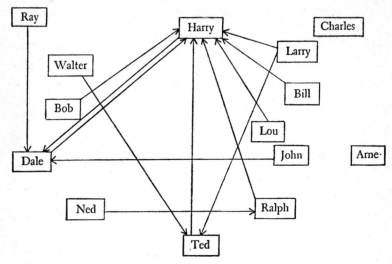

Note: LARRY voted for both HARRY and TED. ARNE and CHARLES did not
express a choice.

through the vote for best leader, while Chart 2 shows W's
own evaluations of the group relationships according to her
observations during the preceding meetings. It is interesting
that RAY was not voted for as the best leader. To W the
reason for this seems a technical one. Since most of the boys
had given him their vote for mayor—which meant to them
the highest office—they did not vote for him again.

The boys took the decisions of the vote very well, and only
ARNE looked hurt. TED said he would let RALPH be probation
officer if he wanted to, since he did not think he wanted to
be one any more. Very soon after the count of votes, each boy
who had been elected started "office." RAY, as the mayor,
made a definite, positive contribution to the group when from
time to time he counted his "citizens," helping to check on
everybody's presence. He did this in a friendly, nonauthori-
tarian manner.

DALE handed W a note saying, "TED on line." W asked
what that meant, and he said TED had not behaved and that

he, DALE, as the policeman, could stand him on line. W asked him whether he thought standing on line was helpful. "Yes," DALE said cheerfully, "it's the only way to keep discipline." "How do you feel when you stand on line?" W asked. TED stood by with a deep scowl and said that it made you furious and "try to do it!" DALE insisted there was nothing to it. TED threw at him that he, DALE, did not have to stand on line as much as the others because he had been at the hospital most of the time. DALE just smiled. W said she thought the purpose of having officers was to keep some order, but that if something serious should happen, we could all get together in a council and discuss the matter.

Chart 2. Group Relations as Seen by the Worker

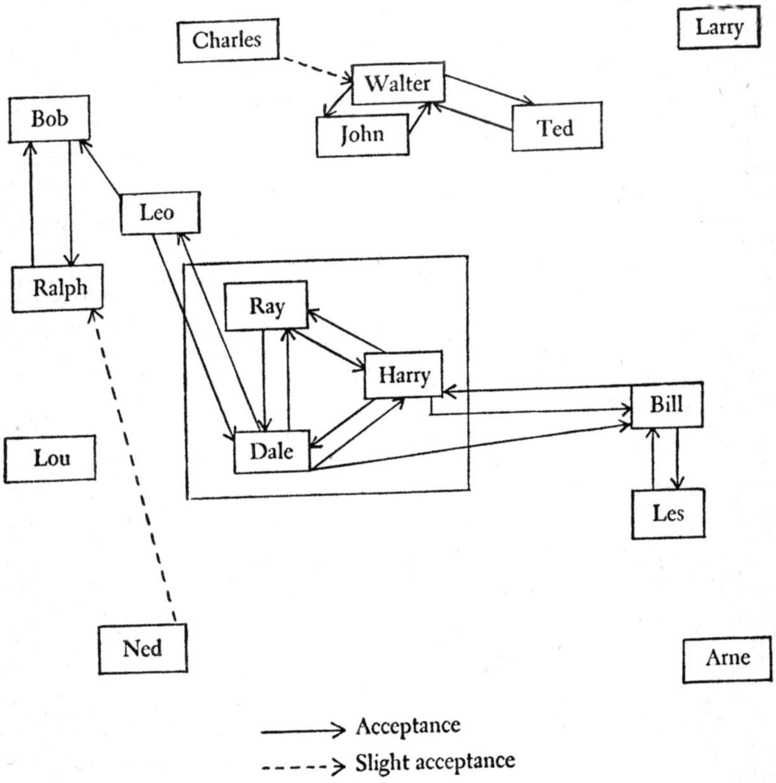

Tenth Meeting

This was the day of the meeting of the Youth Commission, which was to decide the fate of a number of the boys at the reception center. Of W's group, ARNE, LARRY, BOB, BILL, WALTER, and LEO were to appear before the Commission. For ARNE it would be a voluntary reappearance, since no foster home had been found for him during the several months since his previous hearing. The boys were extremely tense, and some of them, including a number of the older boys who were scheduled for hearings, were at a very emotional pitch. Since they were all expecting to be called at any minute, it seemed better to bring some work material downstairs into the basement where they could all remain together, rather than to separate the group.

ARNE was very keyed up, although he said he knew it would not mean training school. He said he did not know what to do, his mind was going around and around. W suggested that he work on something pretty hard, since time goes faster if we have something to do. He took one of the paper plates, asked for a compass, and worked steadily and with great care on an intricate design. He really used his material therapeutically. BOB took some charcoal and drew huge signs that read KEEP OUT and DO NOT ENTER. It struck W again how close to the surface BOB's feelings were, and how frequently he expressed them in symbols. He certainly was afraid today to let himself be wide open.

Since the boys were all together in the basement, W's group along with the other boys, W was better able to observe the natural grouping. It was evident that W's group had developed quite a unity. Although the boys were told they could do what they wanted to, and although many of them were working on different projects, most of them kept together. The only boys who did not stay with the group were BILL, DALE, and RAY. These three did not build a subgroup, either, but joined the older boys. HARRY moved to the older group from time to time also, but most of the time he stayed with W's boys.

At eleven o'clock W left the group in the basement and went to sit in on the hearings of the Commission. The boys who appeared before the Commission took the occasion very seriously. There was not a single one with an "I don't care" attitude. They generally came in subdued and rather afraid, but reacted well to the friendly approach of most of the Commission members. The moment they were attacked, however, they became sullen and withdrawn. It would be interesting to have a camera study of the facial changes that occurred whenever a boy received a scolding; the face that had been frank and open underwent a complete closing-up. This reaction was general. The differences in degree of poise and anxiety were great. One of the older boys seemed on the verge of hysteria and kept his hand around his neck as if he wanted to hold himself in check. At the other extreme was a very poised eighteen-year-old, the only high school graduate in the whole group, who calmly told about his plans to make good— to work, and then to go to a trade school for further training.

It was clear that the moment the boys felt a warm acceptance on the part of a Commission member they were able to talk about what they had done and their plans for the future. The presence of the case worker also meant a great deal to the boys, since they knew and trusted her. To some of the younger ones, the presence of W seemed helpful too, since she was a person who knew them informally and in a pleasant situation.

Eleventh Meeting

At nine o'clock W called the group together. At this point all the boys in the group except Bob knew the decision of the Commission. It had been favorable for most of them—with the exception of Bill—and this made for an unusually happy meeting. Arne, Walter, and Leo had been put on probation and should soon be leaving the center. Plans for Larry's referral to a special school were to be worked out, while the decision on Bob was left for another meeting after further observation. Bill was the only one who had been referred to

the training school. The boys were bubbling over with excite-
ment and joy. They did comparatively little with their hands,
but felt very free to talk. As usual, W will report only the
most significant observations.

WALTER showed the greatest wish to be entirely on the
side of the Commission. He said he could not hold a needle,
he was so excited. He said he liked the men on the Commission so much; they were so nice, and especially Mr. D. He
remembered every word said during his hearing. He said,
laughingly, that he would learn how to avoid the $1.64 which
one member of the Commission had mentioned, and that he
would try to combat "that urge" and get used to not taking
money—all phrases and suggestions that had been mentioned
by the Commission.

LEO was much more outgoing and seemed like a new person.
He said he had really thought he would be sent to the training
school. When W kiddingly said that maybe that was what he
wanted, and that maybe W should have told the Commission so, he said laughingly that he would kill W for that—
a remark that brought forth from the others, "Now you start
already!" When the supervisor later joined the group it was
LEO who especially urged her to be here on the eighteenth,
the day chosen to celebrate the boys' birthdays. He said, "And
be sure you are here, otherwise we will give you four months
here and you will not get before the Commission!" He made
two felt pocketbooks, one for the supervisor and one for W.
He said, "You see, I could not get anything ready before.
What a bit of happiness does!"

LEO spoke with feeling about BILL's going to the training
school. He said BILL had worked so hard on doing well, and
had planned on being so good when he went home. W said
she was sure the Commission realized that too. WALTER said
BILL had had a serious charge against him, pointing a gun at
somebody, and that this was the reason. Somehow the boys
accepted this explanation, because they knew that was a dangerous thing to do. They agreed, however, that BILL had
worked hard at being good, and W said he had a chance not

to stay too long in the training school, if he worked out all right.

The boys then talked about LARRY. LARRY had told them he was going to be sent to a school for the feebleminded. They said he had said he thought that was okay. WALTER said that LARRY had wanted very much to go back to his mother, but that he did not seem to take it too badly. They said that BILL too had been very courageous and had not cried. LARRY himself did not say a thing, just smiled.

Twelfth Meeting

There were few significant incidents during this meeting. Once while the boys were playing ball, the ball fell far off, almost on the street. W asked LARRY to be careful in picking it up. While W walked over to LARRY one of the boys said, "I bet she thinks he wants to drift." And another one answered, "Oh, no, he would never do it when *she* is around—nobody would."

Since the Commission had now made its decisions, W felt it would be desirable to hold a series of discussion meetings with the boys who were about to leave the center, hoping to give them some more direct help in meeting the problems they would face when they got out. With this in mind, W asked the boys if they would like to divide the group, so that there would not be so many of them in one group any more. The boys, however, refused to be separated from each other. It was very interesting to see that a bond had developed in this short time. They said there were not too many of them and they wanted to stay in the same group. W said that she would keep them together if this was what they wanted, but that sometimes in the mornings she would meet separately with the boys who would leave soon, and discuss with them the problems of probation.

Thirteenth Meeting

In the morning W held her first discussion meeting, but in the afternoon the whole group met again. They wished that we had met together in the morning. In general the group showed increased coherence and a stronger group climate. There was less general play but a more relaxed separation into smaller groups.

Since the discussion meeting in the morning HARRY had became much more a participant in the group. Also, a new boy, JOE, had joined the group. JOE gave the impression of having good intelligence and probably more schooling than most of the other boys. In general he was very reserved and appeared to be somewhat on guard against adults. He seemed to team up most with DALE.

We played several games that the boys enjoyed. Some of them involved penalties, usually running toward a tree or having to answer three questions. It was interesting that the questions BOB suggested showed his homosexual fantasies. He would say, "Ask him whether he would like to suck ARNE's toe," or , "Ask him whether he would like to suck somebody's thumb." JOE giggled at these questions, and with this acceptance by one boy, the whole group understood the sex implications. ARNE and TED protested angrily against such questions, and BOB stopped. He never before had come into the open with his problem. It seemed to W that the presence of JOE had stimulated him.

Fourteenth Meeting

W had heard from all the boys, both the older and the younger ones, that Sunday was always a terrible day. They have nothing to do, and they are usually cooped up. One of the seventeen-year-olds said that something should be done about those Sundays! The boys get up at the usual time, have about an hour free in the morning, and go to church from nine-thirty to ten-thirty. On this particular Sunday the boys came back from dinner at about eleven-thirty, but did not leave their basement until one-thirty. It was a very hot day.

The moment W appeared on the scene the younger boys came running toward her. They wanted to be separated from the older ones. W had intended to observe the whole group, but she found the need for separation so crying that she took her group and a few others, a total of sixteen boys. They wanted to do some handicraft, but W suggested that since it was Sunday we should do something else.

W was with the boys for almost four hours, and during this time most of them participated in all kinds of games: straddle ball, guess a word, and others. It was interesting to see how much they enjoyed these not too strongly organized games. They liked most those games in which W told a story or asked funny questions. They needed laughter so badly! They also enjoyed having to answer three questions as a penalty. One of the questions usually asked was whether the boy would like to kiss W. The answer was always a truthful "No," indicating the calm relationship of the boys to W, while the question itself showed their simultaneous wish to play with fire. When ARNE had three questions, the boys suggested that they ask him whether he would like to punch one of the attendants in the nose, and ARNE answered "Yes" with much feeling.

NED was more an isolate at this meeting, only playing catch with one or another of the boys. He got into scraps with almost everyone he played with, and when he was hurt he would sit down and cry and sulk. Some of the boys would wander off from time to time and lie down by themselves. The need for this was very great.

In between games there was some very free talk. The boys by then felt free in W's presence. JOHN, who seems to W one of the most healthy boys in the group, talked about summer school and how he had not gone there, though the judge had ordered it. He was very frank and said he did not think he would ever go now. He did not see why he should spend summer in school. DALE was far more a part of the group this Sunday and really participated. LOU also enjoyed the games and loved to sing for all the others, always calling W's attention to his singing. However, the one who surprised W the most was LARRY. Quite unexpectedly, during a game, W suddenly heard his voice saying clearly and much more reasonably than usual, "Oh, I know this. I learned this in camp." And another time, when W mentioned a country, "I know where that is; I learned it in geography." LARRY really seems to profit during the relaxed periods of these meetings. At such times it is as though he awakens from sleep. The boys often tease him about going to the school for the feebleminded, but he takes it rather calmly. W always mentions that it is just a school and nothing to tease anyone about.

Right after supper W went back to the cottage. The mood of this meeting was, in general, a rather calm one. Most of the boys, with the exception of ARNE, LARRY, and WALTER, sat down and did a lot of singing. W was pleased to see HARRY joining in so well. At one point they all clamored to look through W's glasses, and when W mentioned an eye operation they wanted to hear all about it. Their longing for exciting stories is very great. When W purposely told them of having to lie still for a long time, one boy (W thinks it was LEO) said, "So you can understand what it means, standing on line. You had to be so quiet."

Once a ball rolled across the road and ARNE went to retrieve it. W watched and the boys said again that W was afraid he would drift. W said she was not afraid of that—she was just afraid that somebody might get under a car. "You mean get in a car," said CHARLES. "No," W said, "I do mean under a car." "You *really* like us," said WALTER.

We looked at the sun shining on the bluffs and admired them. W said to LES that he should draw them someday. He smiled and said that they were beautiful at home too. He said he dreamed a lot of home. W wondered why, since he had told her he really did not like his home. He smiled his friendly and patient smile. "No, I don't like home too well, but now I dream about it. It is too long to be here."

Fifteenth Meeting

. . . LARRY started to throw marbles around the floor. W suggested that instead of throwing them around he could put them in a glass and jingle them. He enjoyed that, to the horror of some of the boys, who shouted that he made too much noise. LARRY said triumphantly that W had said he could do it. W supported him, saying that he would stop soon; and he did. . . .

NED, LES, LEO, RALPH, and LOU sat around the table and asked W to tell her story about the war in France. While W told the story there was complete silence. W had seldom seen such attentive faces. W mentioned a boy of their age who had protected his pregnant sister. There was no grinning, no dirty looks. LEO nodded seriously, and they anxiously inquired whether anything had happened to her and the baby-to-come. They begged W to tell more when they met again.

Sixteenth Meeting and Picnic

W had made arrangements with the training school to have a picnic for the whole company, in honor of all the boys who had birthdays during this month. The afternoon was spent in preparations for this picnic. The younger boys felt that they were the committee in charge. W had chosen seven boys to help with carrying food, etc., and they worked hard. W got so tired that she finally asked for helpers among the older boys as well, and quickly six tall, strong boys volunteered.

The picnic was a real success. Several of the boys helped with giving out the food and did a perfect job. The long line formed without any difficulty. The older boys at first seemed quite skeptical about whether there was enough to eat, but as one of them said later, "They sure fooled us! They really got a good picnic together."

The boys sat comfortably in the grass with plates full of good food. Most of them came back for seconds. When they were allowed to reach for the rest of the wieners, W saw only one boy really cheating and taking three instead of one. Even so, when W laughingly called out, "Cheater," he put them back. Cake and ice cream were the climax of the feast.

W had some little gifts for the seven boys whose recent birthdays were being celebrated, and with a bunch of boys collected around her, they all sang a shouting "Happy Birthday." After that they sang "Happy Birthday" to the supervisor, Mrs. X., Mr. F., and Mr. Z. All the staff members whom the boys liked were present, and that added to the enjoyment. Father J. also joined the group later. After this the boys played ball or sat around and talked. All of the staff stayed with them. About ten boys volunteered to help with the clean-up and more would have if they had been asked. They were very ready to help and even suggested that they wash the dishes. It was a really happy evening, and W heard some of them singing while they got ready for the showers.

Seventeenth Meeting

Before this group meeting HARRY approached W and asked whether George, a boy who had just arrived the evening before, could stay with the group, since he was HARRY's best friend. W gladly agreed, knowing that it is an important part of the group worker's role to see and accept special friendships, and then to try to understand their basis and impact.

W told the boys she thought it would be nice if they would write to the people who had prepared food for them at the picnic. To her great surprise LARRY was the first one to say, "I'd like to write to Miss T. [the dietician]." Some of the others objected, saying they were sure he could not write. W said she thought if LARRY wanted to do it, it would be fine if he would. JOE also volunteered to write, and composed a very polite, well-written letter to the superintendent of the training school.

LARRY wrote a long letter, a whole page full. He showed it to W with great satisfaction and said he liked to write long letters. The letter to Miss T. showed his real interest, but also revealed his feeblemindedness and possible schizophrenia. He started out very reasonably: "Dear Miss T., I wish you come tomorrow again." In rather jerky sentences, he wrote all he had on his mind—the picnic, the fact that he is going to go to a school, the meeting of the Commission. Toward the middle of the letter his sentences began to be repeated over and over again. W gave him much recognition, and he asked to write to Miss K. too. He again wrote a whole page and ended up with "Your friend, LARRY." This too he showed W with great satisfaction. When he had finished writing his letters, he started working on a paper plate, making very special designs and showing them to W with joy. (LARRY has shown such progress since these meetings began that W is convinced of the helpfulness of the group work method for feebleminded children. The psychologist later told W that he too had been surprised by LARRY's calling him and talking to him freely.)

W was sitting beside ROGER, a boy who was with the group for the first time. He had reached out for the felt and started sewing. He caught on very quickly, getting real pleasure out of it. He talked freely about himself. He said the trouble was that his family had not gone to Texas. There he would be happy and all right, he said, and his father thought so too. His uncle had died and had left them a little ranch in Texas and a trucking business in Minnesota, and his parents had moved here to look after the trucking business. His father really is a barber and is continuing with that work here. "He really doesn't know a thing about trucking. He has to hire people."

According to ROGER, the police had forbidden him to use a truck, but one of the men got sick and Roger had driven it and been caught. W looked a little skeptical at this, and he added suddenly with a smile, "Oh, there was another matter too. I drove a car that wasn't mine and I ruined it." W talked with him a moment about the fact that the car was not his. He said, with some anger, that it belonged to a cop and that he would destroy anything that belonged to "them." W said it would be good if we could talk a little more about the role of the police.

ROGER spoke with longing about Texas, the horses, and the ranch. His father had promised him the train fare, and he hoped he would be allowed to go there. W asked who would take care of him there and send him to school. There was no clear answer to that, which showed that a great deal of all this was probably wishful thinking. ROGER said he liked it at the center.

A quarrel between JOE and NED broke out at the table. JOE started to tell NED that he shouldn't think he could get out of here just because his father was home—his father was a jailbird anyway. NED looked not only hurt but helpless. W said it seemed strange that JOE should throw that up to NED. Couldn't people change? "Oh," JOE said, "not if they have been in jail." W pointed out that people can be in jail and learn that they have made a mistake, and then become very good citizens. Additional help came from CHARLES, who said that it was not NED's fault, anyhow, that his father had been in jail, and that nobody can help what his parents are. JOE certainly was not convinced, but NED had got the necessary support. (In this incident, the role of protector was first assumed by the worker and was then taken over by one of the boys.)

When it was time to leave, HARRY called the boys together and got them in line. At several other times during the meeting he had also taken on the role of helper, collecting papers, etc. He told W that Mr. K., the chief probation officer, had said he might be home soon. This reassurance did a lot for HARRY, whose distrust and bitterness had become quite marked.

Eighteenth Meeting

. . . It was a hot day, and the wind was blowing without relief. This weather seemed to make itself felt with everyone, and the boys were restless. Things went all right, however, until NED and LARRY got into a fight. Neither boy had any self-control, but LARRY had a real fit and was dangerous. He threw stones and took up the scissors and a large pole. Fortunately, he is not very quick, so W could get hold of him. W held both his arms, talking in a soothing voice until he relaxed under her hands. The difficulty was that NED did not let him alone, but again provoked him. LARRY's rage mounted once more, and besides physical force he used terrible language.

Again he reacted to the holding and the soothing words like somebody coming out of a trance. He then lay down on the ground, completely exhausted, sweat standing on his forehead. When he had rested a little, W asked him if he wanted to draw and write out all his anger. He was perfectly willing to do this, and NED immediately asked for paper too.

When it was time to leave, NED hit LARRY still again and said in an angry voice that he was never, never coming to this group again. W said calmly that that was all right, which did not please him.

Nineteenth Meeting

. . . ROY, a new boy who was in one of W's discussion groups, was looking very unhappy and wore a deep frown. He said dejectedly that it was nonsense to wait here at the center, that they would be committed to the training school anyhow. JOE joined in, agreeing with this attitude. W wondered whether they knew how many boys had gone to the training school and how many had not, after the last Commission meeting. They said yes, they knew that only seven out of twenty-two had gone to the training school, but that it was terrible to wait and not know what would happen to you. (This criticism is important!) They also expressed distrust that the decision of the Commission did not mean a thing. They were very conscious of cases like those of DALE and WALTER, who had been put on probation but were still at the center because no suitable foster homes had been found as yet. W explained about the difficulties of placement. Fortunately, JOHN now joined the group, and he was more positive. He said that certainly the Commission wanted to check on the farmers so that they would not just make the boys work and work.

JOE and ROY asked to have the discussion group meet again. JOE said he had just "spoken his mind," and W said that she appreciated that. JOHN asked whether he could be in a discussion group before W left. He had always attended the regular group meetings very faithfully.

Twentieth Meeting

For the last three days W had met with the whole group together. The group had grown, so that it now included twenty-two boys. Since the group had learned to know W and W to know the boys, far more freedom could be given them—a proof that mutual respect helps a great deal in working out the problem of discipline.

The group of twenty-two spread over a rather large area. In groups of six or seven, some of the boys did handicraft work. A few others played catch or volleyball, since they seldom can use the ball when the older boys are present. Two boys clamored to play on the "monkey bars," which were rather far off. W said they could go there if one of them would take the responsibility for keeping those who went together, and for bringing them back when W called. JOE and WALTER both agreed to be responsible; and in all three meetings when they were at the bars, often with as many as six other boys, they took their responsibility very well.

RECORDS OF DISCUSSION MEETINGS

First Meeting

Five boys who were soon to leave the reception center—
HARRY, WALTER, LEO, BOB, and ARNE—made up this special
discussion group. BOB was included although the discussion
about further plans for him had been postponed. Because of
his severe problems every attention that could be given him
was thought helpful. The discussions were conducted sitting
informally around a table outside the cottage. W started out
by saying that it would be good to discuss a little what would
be waiting for them when they went out from here. W realized, she said, that at the moment going home looked just
wonderful; but there would be some difficulties too, and it
might help to discuss them now so they would be prepared
for them.

W asked the boys what they thought would be especially
difficult. It was interesting that HARRY, who usually speaks
very little, was the first one to react. He said that school
would be the biggest problem. Then all the others, one after
another, said they thought it would be school too.

W: What is it that will be so difficult in school?
HARRY: Mainly the teachers.
W: Well, what about the teachers?
WALTER: Oh, they don't understand you.
LEO: Sometimes you want to explain something and they
    just shut you up.
BOB: They don't like boys; they make it tough on you.
LEO: The man teachers are the worst. They are rough and
    they hit you. Women should work with boys; they under-
    stand them much better.

W wondered what kind of teacher they would like. They

all stated that it should be somebody who liked them and let them explain things and did not teach things so boringly. HARRY said he had known only one teacher whom he really liked. W wondered whether they did not want to go to school. Every single one of the boys said he wanted to go to school and wanted to finish school. WALTER was especially outspoken on this, saying you could not do anything if you did not have schooling. Yet they all showed fear of the teachers. LEO asked whether teachers were allowed to hit their pupils in country schools, and when W said that in some places they were allowed to do this, he looked worried.

W asked the boys what they would do if they felt that a teacher was not treating them right. W granted that this might happen, but pointed out that since we cannot change the teacher, we have to talk about ourselves. What would they do? HARRY said, "Just give them back what they give to you." He had always done that anyhow. LEO agreed heartily, adding that then the teacher might know how it is and change. (W saw with mounting awareness that this is what the boys feel society is doing to them—paying them back for what they did and thereby trying to "change" them.) Yet when W asked, "Will the teacher really change?" the answer came in chorus that no, this would not be the case.

W asked, "Well, what would happen?" BOB said they would be thrown out of school, and HARRY added that this was what had happened to him. W told the boys there was a law that they must go to school until they were sixteen years old, and anyway they had said they wanted to go to school. So it might not be such a good idea to work toward getting thrown out of school. What could they do instead?

WALTER said they could just take it, and anyhow he knew some swell teachers. We then discussed the fact that sometimes we have to learn to get along with people even if we don't think much of them. W told the boys that she thought they might be much more understanding with their own children someday because they had experienced how it feels not to have somebody understand you. But in order to grow up to this, they would have to take some difficulties along the way.

What would help if they felt terribly angry? They said, just somebody to talk to. W wondered if places like settlement houses offered any help. The boys said it would be good to have a place where they could make things and have fun and meet friendly people. HARRY said he had liked X. House much better than Z. House. "Why?" W asked. HARRY answered, "Because this Mr. C.—well, he really cared about us. At Z. House they didn't."

W said to the boys that this remark seemed important—what they wanted most was a person who cared about them and who understood them. Sometimes it is important that they themselves make an effort to find such a person. "Who could it be?" They said, maybe a teacher, or sometimes the foster parents. W finally suggested the probation officer. BOB was the only one to say that he knew a good probation officer, and that he had been able to get things off his chest with him. The others complained that the probation officers had so little time that you could talk only five minutes to them. LEO said he had been in the country, and the probation officer there had to see so many boys in so many different communities that he came only during school hours for a few minutes, and LEO could never talk to him. We discussed further the fact that they should try, when they were really troubled, to talk things over with someone—to make a real point of doing this.

It was about at this point that HARRY asked whether they could also talk about things that troubled them at the center. W said they certainly could, although much of that probably would have to be taken up with the supervisor, Miss K. HARRY, in a groping but persistent way, said he had become very discouraged because although he had been before the Commission a long time ago, and although other boys had left the center, still he was not allowed to leave. ARNE added with great bitterness—during the discussion his voice grew louder and louder until he almost shouted—that he too had been kept here much too long. Others had left but he and

HARRY stayed. The other boys, WALTER and LEO, showed great fear that they also might meet the experience of these boys. They all felt very insecure because a decision made by the Commission did not seem to mean much. They also quoted as examples the cases of Al and DALE. They too had been put on probation, but could not be released because no suitable foster homes had been found as yet.

W felt that there was real justification for the boys' fears and that she should answer realistically. She explained the difficulty of finding foster homes, how people sometimes want just this kind of a boy or just that age. She told them that the Commission and the probation officer do not want to dump the boys just anywhere, but try to find the best place for each one. None of these reasons convinced the boys. Their insecurity is so great that any promise not kept is to them just another proof that people do not mean what they say. Every one of W's explanations was answered by "We would try living anywhere," or "HARRY wants to go to his father, anyhow."

HARRY was calm, but under this calm was something like real despair. He said he would ask to go before the Commission a second time, just as ARNE had done, but that he was afraid to, because he did not want them to decide that he should go to the training school. (How much HARRY distrusts people!) He asked if W couldn't ask Miss K. to do something for him. LEO mentioned several times that cases were not handled in the order they came in, and that those who were here first should be handled first. W explained that it takes time for information about the boys to come in. WALTER supported her here, saying that the Commission should know about each boy's "early life."

ARNE in his excited but very honest way broke out with some of his resentment toward the rules at the center. He said nobody could stand being in a basement with seventy boys all the time. The noise was so great that you had to shout to talk; and, "When you feel bad at home, at least you can leave, but here you go into a corner and soon somebody comes to tease you!" He also objected to being constantly in locked rooms. He said Bennie had told him that he had dreams in which his mother followed him through every room and always locked it after him. He insisted that nothing like this was ever done at the county school, and that it was horrible to sleep in a locked-in place. He complained about the constant lines, not only standing on line, but lining up to go to the toilet, to wash, to do everything. The other four boys, in a less excited way, agreed with ARNE with great bitterness.

W said she was sure that everyone on the Commission would think their complaints justified. She pointed out that this was only an emergency situation because the Youth Commission was young, and that when things are new they are usually not worked out too well. Interestingly enough, this time W's reasons were somewhat better accepted. ARNE knew the date when the Youth Commission started and agreed that it had been operating only a short time. Although not all the bitter feelings were resolved, at least the outburst had helped.

HARRY said he wanted to talk about another problem, smoking. With the exception of WALTER, all the boys agreed that there was no harm in smoking, so why shouldn't they? ARNE said that if you have a habit for four years and you get here, it is not right to take things away. W asked whether, if somebody had the habit of stealing, we should let him go on stealing here? That made ARNE more thoughtful, but his answer was that smoking was not a bad habit. WALTER said that smoking prevents you from growing, and it is better not to smoke until you have stopped growing. ARNE, who at this point was unable to accept any reasoning, insisted that people grow all their lives, so in that case you could never smoke. BOB said, smiling shyly, that he himself had felt that breathing became difficult when he was smoking. LEO said it does not hurt if you don't inhale.

It seemed clear to W that this gripe about not being able to smoke was more an additional expression of dissatisfaction and hostility than an expression of an actual need for smoking.

W, therefore, said that there were different opinions about smoking. It seemed that it was harmful if done in excess, but she wondered whether they felt it was so important, anyhow, if they had other things to do. HARRY said that he felt no urge to smoke when he was outside, only when they were all inside and the older boys got their smoke. W agreed that that must be hard.

Time was up, and W asked the boys whether they wanted to continue the discussion on Monday. They said they wanted to very much. They were extremely reluctant to leave, but W felt she had to send them back so that they weren't given too many special privileges the others did not have.

Second Meeting

W asked whether the boys remembered what we had talked about two days ago. BOB answered at once, "Smoking"—an indication of how important this problem is to him. HARRY said we had talked about teachers too, and how hard it was to find somebody who was understanding. They all repeated how it would be better not to give "meanness back" but to try to get along. They also spontaneously remembered the probation officer as somebody to turn to.

W wondered whether there were other difficulties they would have to face when they got out. ARNE said one difficulty would be the people at home who would ask so many questions about where they had been. DALE, who was with the discussion group for the first time, BOB, and WALTER were all reasonably sure that they would not go back into the same environment as before, but they all agreed that people might ask them questions at the new place too, and anyhow, they hoped to visit at home. (Several times WALTER asked anxiously whether they would be allowed to stop at home at least for a day. W said that he should take that up with Miss K.) They all agreed that it was a tough problem to face people. W asked, "Why?" BOB said slowly, "Because it is a disgrace." HARRY added, "It is, and they always think it's your mother's fault." ARNE said, "I have older brothers and they feel disgraced."

> W: Let's think for a moment what that means. What is really the disgrace? To be here?
>
> DALE: Oh, really the things we have done, but people think differently.

W suggested that first we should stick to what we thought. WALTER said that this was really a place that wanted to help them to get along better. W said they knew this was not a jail. They understood, they said, but ARNE said with feeling that they were closed up, anyhow, and beaten, and people don't always understand. The discussion almost turned into another session about the reception center, so W suggested to the boys that this time we should stick to our difficulties and the problems we would meet on leaving here.

> ARNE: Yes, let's do that. Now, for instance, there is a man in a drugstore at the corner. I don't know whether he likes me and is interested in me or if he is mean and wants to tease me. Every time I come back he right away asks me where I have been, why I went there, and so on. It makes me mad.
>
> W: What do you answer, ARNE?
>
> ARNE: It's none of your business.
>
> WALTER: Well, that will make him really mad at you.
>
> W: What would you answer, WALTER?
>
> WALTER: I was at the YCC because I got into trouble, and now I know better and will get along.
>
> W: What do the rest of you think?
>
> HARRY: That won't make him so mad, but he will ask more.
>
> W: Let's think for a moment why this man and other people might ask such questions.
>
> ARNE: He wants to know.
>
> DALE: He is jealous.
>
>> (The others laughed, "What should he be jealous about?")
>
> DALE: I can't explain, it just seems to me . . .

W: Maybe Dale has something there—wait a minute. And what do the others think?

Bob: He is curious.

(The others agreed with this.)

W: Have you ever seen what people do when they see a soldier coming home with one arm?

Bob: Sure, they always ask questions. And the soldier might not want to talk about it, either.

Arne: They are not really mean, they are just curious.

W: Sure. You see, people are that way. Your drugstore man probably does not know it, but maybe he would like some attention too.

(This was the first time W had given the boys a more complicated interpretation of feelings. They listened very attentively, Arne and Walter nodding gravely. W is not sure that they really understood, but thought it helpful not to drop Dale's remark entirely.)

Bob: So it is better to give some friendly, steady answer.

W: Do you think you boys can try that now?

Arne: I think I can, but it is tougher with the kids. They really tease you.

Harry: Sure, they make you feel miserable. They ask, Where have you been? What did you do? What do they do to you? Do they beat you? Do you get enough to eat? Tell us all about it.

Arne: Harry knows. Harry went through it once.

W: Why do you think the boys ask?

Dale and Bob: Oh, they're curious too.

Arne: And it sounds exciting.

W: Sure. They like adventure, and it is like an adventure story to them. What do you do when they tease you?

Arne: Oh, I get mad, really mad.

Walter: That won't help, Arne.

W: Let's try it. One of you tease the other and he will answer.

(The boys all refused to be the teaser, fearing the other boy would really get mad at him.)

W: Okay, I'll tease ARNE and he'll answer.

W does not recall the exact words of the dialogue that followed, but she repeated the things the boys had said, asking ARNE where he had been, and calling him a good-for-nothing. ARNE always answered defiantly, getting more and more angry until he was reduced to an incoherent "You . . . you . . ." W stopped at this point and asked what would come next? They all shouted that now a fight would come. One of them added, "And being on probation, that might end badly for you, ARNE."

W asked whether someone else would like to try. WALTER was willing, and this time ARNE was the teaser. This dramatization was unusually realistic. ARNE used every possible mean device. After he had asked the usual questions, he started with a dry, "Well, you won't go straight. You started little and you'll get worse. You'll end in the reformatory anyhow."

WALTER stuck to his guns with an amazing calm. He always answered clearly, and he gave a good interpretation of the Youth Conservation Commission. He said he *tried* to go straight. To the reformatory attack, he said, "Maybe, but I'll try not to." At another point, after ARNE had attacked him with, "I bet you can't go straight for three days," he said, "I've been out for three weeks and I'm still all right."

ARNE: Oh, three weeks. Your parents probably kept you at home all the time. You're only good when you're in bed.

WALTER: I went to school, didn't I?

ARNE: Your poor mother—what she has to take!

WALTER: We're getting along all right now.

W stopped the dramatic play at this point. The others discussed it, saying it was helpful to get it so clearly in mind. They would try to act the way WALTER did in the play. W said she knew it would be harder when the teasing was real, but she hoped it would help to have thought it through a little, and maybe, in the middle of the teasing, they might remember our discussion.

ARNE said it would help too if everybody went to church on Sunday. He had seen boys stealing while people were in church. He added, with bitterness, that they were not caught. Some of the other boys felt the cops had just "picked on" them. W wondered whether the stealing itself was exactly right, even if they were not caught. ARNE said he had seen people bringing things for a crippled child in their cars, and some boys had stolen the things. That was really mean! The others thought so too.

HARRY said there was another kind of teasing too. When you want to stay out of trouble the boys call you "Mama's baby" and say you are a sissy. "That makes you mad," HARRY said. DALE agreed wholeheartedly and said nobody could call him a sissy. This led to a discussion of what it means to be a sissy. Not to be able to stand up against others, the boys said. Well, that meant standing up too against the boys who called you sissy. And what were they doing? ARNE said they often would not dare to do the things they dared you to do. W said, "Well, who is the sissy?" HARRY said the others, because they made you take the blame. W said that was the point, that we shouldn't let ourselves be provoked by others. W also told them about a sailor she knew who had always been teased about not drinking; yet he was stronger than the others, and soon they found that out and admired him. (This was a difficult part of the discussion. To W it seemed a subject that must be discussed again, since it is very hard for these boys to be called sissy. Their own egos are so weak that they need constant reassurance that they really are "strong.")

At times the cars that were passing on the road were more interesting to the boys than the discussion. WALTER, especially, was often distracted. When he got too excited about them, W interrupted the discussion, saying it seemed that a few minutes to admire the cars were necessary. This usually helped, and soon the conversation could go on again.

Toward the end of the meeting the boys wanted to talk

about school again for a moment. Bob said he hated school, yet when we compared where everybody was in his grade placement, Bob seemed farthest ahead, if his own information was right. Arne and Walter tried to convince the others that they should finish high school. Arne said he had told the Commission that he wanted to finish high school, and he would stick to his word—he had meant it. When W asked why they thought school was important, Harry said that if you have no schooling, people can cheat you everywhere—you couldn't count your money in a store, and you couldn't read. Bob said that he could do farming, but Walter said that you need to know all those things as a farmer too. W underlined this, pointing out how many skills a farmer must have nowadays. Walter repeated, "It's a highly skilled job."

Dale seemed farthest back in school. He said that summers were terrible for being in school. He likes to go out in the woods and shoot rabbits. W gave him recognition for his adventurous spirit, but said that there are a few things all of us must do, even if we don't like them too much.

It was time to close. The boys wanted to stay on, but W said they could continue the next day. Bob had been rather quiet. He said that recently he had been thinking and thinking, but that he likes to figure things out for himself. He said he might share his ideas with us later.

Third Meeting

It was the day of the picnic, and W told the group that she would need two boys to help her with buttering the rolls in the kitchen that afternoon. There was much clamoring for this work, and W selected Arne and Bob. This led to an outburst by the other boys, under the leadership of Harry, saying that Bob was too dirty to work with food. While Bob turned red with shame, they said that nobody wants to sit beside him at the table, because he does not wash. When he gets a package, they said, nobody wants to eat his stuff. W wondered what Bob had to say. He quite evidently knew the boys were right, and said he would try to do better. Harry said somebody should use a scrub brush on him. Bob said, "Okay, I'll let one of you scrub me today." Harry got angry and said he should be able to do that for himself. W asked whether they couldn't be a little helpful to each other; couldn't somebody have told Bob earlier? Harry said he had told Bob right in the beginning, and added, in a very grown-up manner, that once when Bob had washed, well, he just looked like a changed boy. Bob insisted that he would scrub, really scrub, this afternoon before W called him, if W would only let him have a chance. W told him she believed he would do it and she would stick to her decision to let him help in the kitchen.

At this point Mr. D. came to call Bob for an interview. When he left, W asked the boys whether they thought they could be of some help to Bob. They said they just wished he were not so dirty. W told them that Bob never really had any parents, and how do people learn to keep themselves clean? Walter answered quickly, "From their parents." W explained how hard it is to learn all kinds of things if you have nobody to take care of you. Harry said somebody must have raised Bob, he sometimes gets packages, doesn't he? W said that certainly he had been with all kinds of families, but that was not the same thing. Packages did not mean that anybody had made a home for him and taught him the things he should know. After this the boys were quite thoughtful and more friendly toward Bob.

Then followed an outburst of dammed-up hostility. They talked about the "jail" here. When W said it seemed better than a jail to her, they said—and they were all rather outspoken, with the exception of Walter—that jail was much better. When you were in your cell in jail you could do what you wanted to, but here you were watched every minute. "Mr. W. [one of the attendants] says, 'You must play.'" (W had heard that herself.) They said that in jail they would not have to sit with seventy people all the time in a damp basement. People were constantly locking up behind them here—wasn't that the same as in jail? In jail the attendants would not be allowed to beat them, but here anybody could beat them when he wanted to. When W took the group it was "heaven," but who else let them out or trusted them? Like a refrain, Mr. W. was mentioned over and over again.

W asked what they thought of Mr. G., another attendant. "Oh, he is swell. If everybody were like Mr. G. it would be okay." And Mr. M. and Mr. N., two of the housefathers? They liked them too. W said to the boys that maybe it was really not so bad here, that they were just very angry at one person. And that showed us, just as in school and on the playground, that *people* are important. Slowly the discussion moved away from the direct outpouring of hostility. W wondered whether they themselves didn't fly off the handle sometimes. Were they sure they would treat *their* children better? Arne said a licking might be good. This was very much objected to by Harry and Walter, and W agreed with them. We talked a little about how we could raise a boy without licking him.

There seemed to be little point in discussing the probation period at this time, and since almost an hour had passed, W suggested that we join the rest of the group.

Fourth Meeting

W told the four boys—Leo and Bob were not present—that this would be their last discussion group, since they would soon be leaving. W summarized briefly what we had talked about and asked if this time we could talk about each boy separately, and look at what his situation would be and what he himself could do to get along better.

Arne asked whether he would be allowed to smoke while on probation. W said that the rules would be different for different boys, and that they should ask those definite questions when they met their probation officers. Did any of them know any other probation rules? Harry said that they would have to be home at a certain time and go to school. He said that he had once violated probation. Walter did not understand the word "violation," and Arne translated it for him as breaking probation, getting into trouble again. We discussed the fact that breaking probation was a very serious thing.

HARRY's situation came under discussion first. He was not sure yet where he would go, but he was sure it would be back in town. W asked him about his plans. He said he would go to school, but that he wanted to quit when he was sixteen years old. He did not want to be a paper boy. W said that it might be a good idea to think out right in the beginning what he could do when he was out of school. HARRY said he didn't know—there was nothing that interested him especially. He thought his father might help him find something. W told HARRY that we could be very frank among ourselves, and maybe he thought there was not much use in trying anything because he is a Negro. He said that is what many people say. W said that he could always try, and that many more jobs are opening up for Negroes. She mentioned an organization which was formed especially to help Negroes get better jobs— the Urban League. All the boys listened seriously and with interest. W mentioned George Washington Carver. HARRY and ARNE had heard of him but they did not know who he was. WALTER suddenly said he was an inventor. W told them about him, and remarked that probably none of us would be a genius—there was a big smile from HARRY—but we could try our best.

ARNE said he would be on the road during the next two weeks with his older brother. The boys wondered whether probation would allow this. W said she did not know but thought it was important to check. ARNE thought it would be all right because his older brother would be there to take care of him, and it would only be until school started. W said that he should remember that outside nobody would watch him every minute, and that it would be important for him to take responsibility for his own behavior. WALTER added, "Just don't take somebody else's money or Cadillac or bicycle." ARNE said that he thought he could be pretty sure he wouldn't, and that he wanted to finish school and become a good worker.

WALTER was the next one. He said he would do farm chores and go to school. He wanted to finish school. W wondered if he would know what to do with himself when he was not working, in the evenings and on holidays. (HARRY had mentioned a new settlement house playground.) WALTER said he might visit his parents, and on Sunday morning he would always go to church. ARNE said he would too. WALTER thought he might sometimes play with the kids outdoors, and then, too, he had learned about hobbies. He wanted to have more hobbies in the future.

DALE asked him why he had run away from the farmer he stayed with the last time. WALTER said the farmer had not let him visit his parents and had called his father bad names. He also had not let him go to church, and had said that WALTER's parents put dumb thoughts in his head. One day he had put his good trousers on, hidden behind the barn, and run away. W added, "And that was not really smart, was it?" WALTER said he was caught, anyway. W wondered what he would do if he got angry at Mr. O., the farmer with whom he was hoping to be placed this time. WALTER said that would not happen there. W persisted, saying that things looked lovely now, but there might be a time when he would not like it. He said he would go to his room and think it over, and then he would probably feel better. W thought this was a good idea, but wondered whether other things might not help too. HARRY said, "Talk to the probation officer." W said that was what she meant. Maybe the probation officer would not be available right away, but WALTER could wait with his anger and then talk it over. In the worst case, there was always the possibility of calling the Youth Commission and telling them he needed help. They again talked very seriously about these possibilities.

DALE was less sure than the others where he would be, and he felt a little unhappy about this. W said that he probably would know soon, and that she was sure Mr. K. (the chief probation officer) was working on it. He said he would go to school, although he did not like it. He hoped to work on the farm; he liked the animals best. He was not much interested in talking about home.

W told the boys that the most important thing for them to know was that now their life depends on *them*. They nodded. ARNE said, "If I feel the rage coming up, I'll press my hands together and it will remind me." W had once suggested this to him as a help when he had a tantrum.

We then closed the meeting to join the others.

GROUP II

First Meeting

W decided to try a new discussion group, since the one for the boys who would soon go out on probation had worked so well. This time W wanted to see what such a discussion group could do for newcomers. Almost invariably the new boys felt very insecure. They heard the other boys talking about the Commission, but they were not sure what it meant and they felt left out.

W asked five newcomers—ROGER, JOE, HERB, GUS, and ROY—to come to a group in the morning. All five of these boys had attended at least one of the informal meetings of the general group, and therefore knew W somewhat. This prerequisite seemed very important to W.

At this meeting W and the boys sat around a table out-of-doors. W told the boys that she had asked them to come for an hour's discussion because she thought they probably had a lot of questions on their minds. W said that we could be very frank with each other here, and that the more openly we discussed things the more helpful it would be. After today they could decide for themselves whether they wanted more of this.

GUS started the ball rolling by asking what W's group was all about. W explained in as simple terms as possible that we thought it would be helpful not to have all the boys crowded together all the time and that W also had found that it was good to have a few hours each day when the boys could decide on their own activities and make some of their own decisions. They would have to do this later on too, when they left the reception center. W asked them whether there was anything they would specially like to do. If so, W would try to provide it. Suggestions came thick and fast from all five of the boys, mainly requests for handicrafts. Lastex work and making rings out of plastic were at the top of the list. W was interested to see that a real need for such work was expressed.

W asked whether there were other ways in which they needed help too. Roy said hesitantly that he would like to know what YCC meant, and why they were here. Herb joined in, saying he did not understand the whole thing. W asked if anyone had explained to them the Youth Commission setup. Hadn't the judges told them? Their faces were blank. W asked each one what the judge had said when he had suggested their coming to the YCC reception center. Herb's answer was typical of all the rest: "He looked at some magazine and he looked at a big book and he said 'YCC,' and I was brought here." (It is perfectly possible that the judges gave a much more detailed explanation. This shows, however, how upset the boys are at this point, and how often they need more information.)

W explained what the Youth Commission is, how the new law tries to help youngsters like them, and how their stay at the reception center was just a period of learning to know them, so that then a decision could be made as to what would be best for them. Roger and Herb asked why, since this was not a punishment, they were allowed to be beaten by the attendants, and why they were constantly locked in and watched. The others joined in on this, saying how terrifying the locking-in was, especially at night. W said that beating was not allowed and that they should let Miss K. know when it happened. The locking-up, W said, was mainly because the officials were afraid that some of the boys might run away. W said that neither she nor anyone else working there thought that everything was perfect, but that W thought they were old and intelligent enough to know that things do not always work out in the best way. W told them how new the YCC

was, and explained about the lack of funds. It was interesting
that the boys listened attentively, sometimes nodding assent.
  Joe suddenly said in a bitter tone of voice that the whole
thing was nonsense, anyhow—they would all go to the training school, and even if they were put on probation, they all
would be back someday. W asked Joe why he thought this?
In the same bitter tone he said that they all were no good
anyhow, that he knew they would do the same things they
did before. He would too. (Joe's bitterness was pathetic. He
was one of the most intelligent boys at the center and apparently very hurt. He needed much help.) The other boys, especially Herb, objected. "No, we will not do it again."

> Gus: Sometimes you do things because you had a raw deal.
> W: Hm, there are reasons why we do these things. What
> happened to you, Gus?
> Gus: Well, everything would be okay now, I would have a
> new family, if I had not been caught. You know, I ran
> away from another boys' school and I got along all right.
> I slept on the roofs and I met Arthur in a movie. Arthur
> is such a swell boy. And he took me home and his family
> would have adopted me.
> W: Do you know anything about your parents, Gus?
> Gus: (He was apparently relieved that he could talk more
> about himself, and poured out his whole story.) No, I
> don't know my father. But I have a mother, I have a
> mother. But I lived in a convent. And the sisters said
> I had set a fire, but I didn't. I wish they didn't say things.
> I didn't set the fire. I ran away from the convent and
> later I ran away from the school.
> Roger: He did have a raw deal. He has no parents. I have
> parents. I didn't have a raw deal, but I stole a car. Lots
> of boys do, only I got caught.
> W: If you were not caught, then the car stealing would be
> all right, Roger?
> Roger: I don't know.

W: Would you like it if you had a car and somebody stole it from you?

JOE: I would, if I had insurance. I would be glad if somebody stole it.

HERB: You're crazy, JOE. He might have to go somewhere fast and the car is gone. And it is wrong anyhow. You should not steal.

(Here ROY, who usually was very quiet, nodded.)

HERB: I sure will never take a car again. Only I'm so worried about my mother. She had intended to move to California and now she can't because I'm here. What will happen to us?

Now the conversation turned again to the reception center. ROY said that nobody trusts them here. W said this was not quite the case. W said she trusted them, and she was sure the Commission members and Miss K. did too. Didn't they feel it when they talked to one of them? GUS said earnestly that he had talked to Miss K. and he liked her, but he could not say yet whether she trusts him or he trusts her. W said she respected that, that it takes time to really trust a person. GUS came back to his wish to have parents. He said he wished he could be put on probation. W asked what he would do if he were. Oh, he said, he had met ARNE here, and ARNE would be his friend and take him home to his parents, and they would adopt him. (It was touching to see how strong GUS's wish for parents was. He reached out wherever he could.)

The mention of ARNE led the group into a discussion about their own relationships to other boys. All the boys, with the exception of GUS, said they could not stand ARNE, that he fought too much. W thought it might help if they understood ARNE's difficulty. W said that ARNE had a hard time controlling his temper, that was *his* difficulty, while other people have other difficulties. For instance, some people are fat and others tease them about it, yet they can't help being fat. W was interrupted by JOE's angry and biting comment, "Sure, they are nuts in their brains and therefore eat too much." W continued that it was not one's brains but one's glands—she explained this further—and being fat had nothing to do with being "nuts." (W had brought this subject up because she knew the boys were constantly teasing one of the boys who was very heavy.) W then pointed out the parallel case of ARNE's outbursts of temper. HERB said, "It makes sense. Sometimes you can't help doing things, only you must learn." W was amazed by the way the others also understood.

W said she wondered whether they could not help each other to get along better. ROY said that if they tried to get along, the other boys called them "sucko," which meant a kind of teacher's pet. W asked who was called that. "Dave, JOE, and myself," he said. W asked the boys what they thought of Dave, an older boy. "He's a swell guy," they all answered. Well, W said, then they didn't have to worry if some people called him or them "sucko." As long as a person really is all right, names do not mean too much.

JOE had turned his back during this discussion. W asked him why he was so bitter. Didn't he like anybody?

JOE: No, I don't. The person I like is my mother.
ROGER: What about your father, JOE?
JOE: (In a low voice) He's dead. He got killed by a car.
GUS: That's tough. I have nobody.
HERB: And my parents are divorced. I just wanted to see my father. I wanted to run away where he was, in Chicago.
ROGER: My parents are alive, but they always quarrel. I wish grownups would not quarrel so much. I knew some good people. They will feel sad that I'm here. I wish I could write them.
W: Why don't you ask Miss K. about that, ROGER? She probably will give you permission.
ROY: (Quietly) My family is okay. (This is interesting since the charge against ROY is that he threatened to kill his father.) Grown people are not so good, either. And the police are mean.

(There was general agreement that they were mean, while W tried to defend the police.)

ROY: What about the sheriff who brought me here and got drunk all along the way? Should I have respect for him?

W: I know people are not perfect. In fact, maybe you can be much better than these adults because you have gone through this experience. Do you think that every one of us adults is always perfect?

GUS: (With real conviction) Oh, no.

W explained that everybody makes mistakes, but that this need not mean the end of their lives.

The boys wanted to continue, but our time was up. They asked for another discussion meeting later.

Second Meeting

The first discussion meeting had served the purpose of loosening up the boys. Three main topics had been discussed: the boys' backgrounds, which led to a beginning understanding of their own acts as having some cause; their relationships with other boys, with an attempt to understand other boys' problems; and their relationships to adults, especially those in authority, such as parents, police, and the Youth Commission. At the beginning of the second meeting W briefly summarized these topics.

HERB started out by saying that the indecision was the worst part of being at the center. It was too long not to know what would happen to you, and then, too, school would be starting very soon, and school is very important to him. He was interrupted by ROGER, who complained about the work here; but when W asked if they worked too much, they agreed that they did not. ROY insisted that there was not enough work. He was used to heavy farmwork, and here he was cutting beans. They complained about being too crowded, about people staring at them, about being punished for spilling some food on the table at lunch, and about being hit. GUS said that another institution he had been at had been better. He had only run away because the boys made the rules there, and "The boys they don't like get hell. And, imagine, now they want to introduce that here too!"

It was clear that a short period for griping of this kind was necessary, because the grievances accumulate. When they had got all this out, W suggested that now we could talk about ourselves. She said that some things here really should be changed, but that some conditions just have to be that way in a place where many people are together; and somehow they themselves had brought it about that they were brought here, hadn't they? At this point HERB again picked up the conversation. He said he felt it was his fault that he was here. He had stolen a car. He added, "I always wanted to be a lawyer, but with this against me, I will never make it." W reassured him by saying that he was not "convicted," and that life was still open for him. He was also worried about school, and W said that he wouldn't miss too much. JOE said fiercely that he too wanted to get back to school, but that he would never go back in the middle of the term—what would the others say? W discussed with the boys the difficulty in facing others after leaving the center, and, as in the other group, we talked over what they could say, pointing out the fact that they had not been in a reform school.

JOE said he had taken cars too, and that he hoped he could finish school. He wanted to be a radio mechanic. The tone of his voice was cynical, as usual, but there was a beginning of a more positive reaction. GUS said he had stolen a bicycle and that was not right, but that everything would be all right if he only had a family.

ROGER: I stole a car. Funny, all of us have taken a car or so. Most kids would not be here if it were not for cars.

W: That is interesting, ROGER, isn't it? It would help us if we could understand why we do this. When did you start thinking about taking a car?

This question was put to all the boys, and all except ROY said they began when they were about thirteen years old.

(During all this Roy sat silent, looking very unhappy. He said he would never tell why he came here. W said that was all right. Did he want to leave the group? No, he wanted to stay, but he didn't want to talk. He was told that this was all right too.)

W said to the boys that it was interesting they had all started taking cars around the same age. They nodded thoughtfully. W then explained in very simple terms about adolescence, without using the word. W said that at that age both boys and girls get somewhat restless. Things change, and they are not really children any more. Because they are restless, they want to do a lot of things—"and go fast," added Roger. W said he had hit it on the head. And going fast and having adventure were connected with cars these days. W said that it might be also that they wanted to impress a girl. Herb said with astonishment, "How did you know?" W said it was not so unusual; at that age we all like to impress the other sex. Herb said the girls want a fellow with a car, and he felt so lonely. He again mentioned his parents' divorce. W said she knew it was hard feeling lonely. Gus said he was all alone, but he wanted to find a girl who did not need a car to love him. He said this very seriously. Roger said he knew one who did not mind a fellow without a car, but sometimes he felt alone too. Joe said it was tough when your father was dead. These boys who usually pretend to be tough, especially Joe and Roger, could now frankly admit that they often felt lonely and scared.

W said that being lonely sometimes makes you do things which you later regret. Maybe we could try to find some things and people who would help us get through such lonely times. Herb said that maybe these days at the center had helped him a little; he understood things better. He added, "And I will go back to my mother. I know now that I can't have both of my parents."

W explained to the boys that she had only a few days left at the center, and that she hoped they would not have to wait too long for a decision on their cases.

The boys then joined W's regular group. Before the others came, however, W had a few minutes alone with Roy. He was terribly depressed because of the lack of freedom at the center. He said he still did not know why he was here. He knew he had violated probation, but he didn't know how. He never had to report to anyone. He might have stayed out too late. He said he hated to see people, he feels so ashamed, and all the time he talked his eyes twitched nervously.

INDIVIDUAL CONTACTS

It seemed very important to W to give ROY some additional help before she left. On one of her last days at the center she had to move her luggage from her room in the main building to the home of Mr. F., the superintendent. W asked ROY and HERB to come and help her. When the two boys were called they did not know for what, and W saw the fear in their faces. W met them at the top of the stairs, explaining to them what she wanted and asking them if they would be willing to help. W has seldom seen such relief. Both boys were rather quiet while walking over the grounds, although ROY said several times, "I feel different. I never walked like this over the grounds without a guard." W asked if he minded that she was with them. "No," he said, "that's not the same thing. You don't watch us." (This is very significant, since objectively W's presence was certainly the same as anyone else's.)

Mrs. F. met the boys in a very friendly way, and when they had finished putting the luggage away she cut some pieces of cake for them. HERB was polite in his "Thank you." ROY did not say a single word and hardly lifted his eyes. On the way back he said in a low voice, "I didn't think she was *that* kind."

In the group meeting later ROY showed W a magazine picture of a motorbike, saying he had one like that at home. He talked about the big farm they have, and how he helps with the work and goes to school. He inquired about the country around us and described his countryside back home. He showed a definite loosening up.

On W's last day at the center, she asked ROY in the early afternoon whether he would like to help her with the clean-up. As usual, he was very happy to be allowed to do something like that. He worked well and efficiently, but was bursting with wanting to talk. He sometimes stopped working and

83

just talked and talked. There was a great change in him. His parents had come to visit him and that had meant a lot. Apparently, he had greatly feared their rejection. They had brought him a little radio and that helped him to spend his time with some of the more quiet boys.

He told W all this, and again asked questions about the Youth Commission. The Commission members had arrived that day, and as usual the air was electric, as far as the boys were concerned. W explained to him that the Commission members were very human, and that there was nothing to be afraid of. He fumbled, then burst out with one of his great worries. He had heard that they asked the boys about their plans for the future. Well, he just wasn't sure whether he wanted to be a minister or an electrical engineer. And if he said he wanted to be a minister and later he changed, they would say he had lied, wouldn't they? His sincerity and fear and helplessness in this situation were pathetic. Again it was evident how much someone is needed who is constantly on the premises and who can help with problems as soon as they come up.

W explained to Roy that nobody expected the boys to make definite arrangements for their lives. He could tell the Commission his ambitions just as they were. He asked whether W thought it ridiculous that he considered being a minister. W said she did not think that at all. He took a well-worn pamphlet from his pocket and said earnestly that it explained his church, the Reformed Church. He said that he could not agree completely with the service given by the Lutheran chaplain here, and it worried him. It was not what his church thinks is right. W asked whether he thought it would make much difference when he is thinking of God? He thought for a moment, then said with some astonishment, "Probably not. I can think and pray the way I want." W gave him reassurance on that. He tried to give W the history of the Reformed Church, then told her about some of his classes in electrical work.

At this point Mr. D., the director of the Youth Commission, came into the room. W felt this was a good opportunity for Roy to meet one of the Commission members in an informal way. W introduced him and Mr. D. talked in a friendly way to him. W saw how Roy tightened up again and how his tic became stronger, but he was more able to talk than previously. He even asked Mr. D. whether he knew why he was here. Judge B., another Commission member, arrived and made friendly comments about the ring Roy was wearing, inquiring how it was made. All this meant a great deal to the boy and reaffirmed W's belief that it would be helpful if the Commission could have some informal contacts with the boys. It relieves the boys' fear and helps them to act more naturally.

Roy commented later on how human they were. He said he could wait a little better now. While he was helping W carry things he talked more freely and smiled several times. Crossing the campus we met several staff members, all of whom greeted W in a friendly way. W said smilingly to Roy that before leaving she would tell him a secret: if you smile at people they usually smile back, and if you like them, they almost always like you. He laughed softly and said, "Well, you saw me smile today, didn't you?" He then joined the rest of the group.

CONCLUSIONS

One month of work is too short a time on which to base any claims as to the value of this work in regard to its basic goal—helping the individual boy. We think that even this short program gave some help to these boys; yet only a long-range follow-up could determine this with certainty. Nevertheless, it was evident that during the period of this experiment the boys participating in this special group showed a greater ease than did the others in adjusting to their present situation. Some general observations could be made which in the long run might give us a better understanding of work with all kinds of groups, and improve our methods of dealing with groups of youngsters in institutions.

Concerning the Activity Meetings

In the introduction to the records it was pointed out that the need for intelligent grouping seems paramount in any kind of therapeutic group work. We know comparatively little about this, and each experiment can add only a little to our knowledge. In this case it was found that the rigid routine and the demand for conformity in an institution made natural grouping rather difficult to observe. The less the opportunity for individual expression the smaller was the cohesion of groups or subgroups.

This observation seems very important. It shows a direct correlation between a restrictive atmosphere and a poor esprit de corps, and between a more democratic approach and a closer group adhesion. Many institutions regret the poor group spirit among their youngsters and try to force it upon them by persuasion or special events. But it seems that more individual freedom and more latitude in the choice of friends will do more to help to establish a stronger group feeling. This effect could be observed in the group which met regularly and in a more informal way than the rest of the boys. It was expressed in their wish to stay together when the group increased, in spite of their large number. Group feeling was also indicated by the fact that these boys stayed pretty much together, even when in the larger group, and by the boys' repeated statements that they would not run away while they were with this group.

In the smaller group that W worked with regularly, more natural subgrouping could be observed because of the greater freedom given the boys. It seems interesting that natural grouping did not occur according to the clinical pictures of the boys. Neurotic did not necessarily join neurotic, nor dull-aggressive attract dull-aggressive. Bob, the homosexual, might have been expected to pair off with another boy, according to his clinical diagnosis. Yet in the social area he was almost constantly an isolate. Subgroup cohesion depended mostly on the social attractiveness of the boy.

What seemed to be the criteria according to which sub-groups developed?

(1) One factor was age—not exclusively, not always, but to a large degree. We often think that age grouping is unimportant because we know the differences in intellectual and emotional maturity. Yet, spontaneously, the youngsters themselves put value upon the factor of age. It means to them more than the counting of years. To them, age means mainly status, having more privileges—like smoking, for instance. Being older usually means being stronger, having had more adventure, knowing more girls. Age, therefore, is a symbol of their struggle for status in the group. This explains why some of the physically stronger boys move in easily with the older age group, and why the exceptionally small boy often becomes either an isolate—NED for example—or must pretend to be unusually tough, as in the case of one of the smallest boys, who arrived at the reception center in a fighting mood.

(2) Similar reactions toward adults seemed to be a bond which created subgrouping. In the subgroup composed of RAY, DALE, BILL, and HARRY this seemed to be the common denominator. Each boy was very different from the others,

yet they all had in common a certain attitude toward adults. They were not unusually suspicious, and not especially outgoing, but had a reserved, polite attitude toward adults. This distinguished them from the other boys, who either needed adult attention badly and wanted affection, or were basically hostile. In back of their attitude, distrust and hostility were also present, but they expressed these feelings in an acceptable manner, and somehow this brought them together.

(3) Similar interests brought about temporary subgroups. This seemed to be the weakest bond on which any subgroup formed. The boys who were especially interested in active games, for instance, would be together quite often, but their subgroup showed little emotional cohesion. The same applied to the two boys especially interested in handicraft. They would be together for hours, but there was little carry-over of their relationship when the specific activity discontinued. This bears out the experience of many educational and recreational agencies. Interest groups can meet for a long time without forming a real group bond.

(4) Intellectual differences did not mean too much in grouping. The two feebleminded boys, LARRY and LOU, were isolates and little accepted by the others, but where the margin of difference in intelligence was not so great, it made little difference in social acceptance.

(5) In this setting, subgrouping according to aggressiveness or withdrawal, which has been observed in many other groups, did not appear. This seemed an unusual phenomenon. It may be explained by the restrictive climate of the institutional setting, in which the aggressor, in general, must dam up his aggressive tendencies, and the more withdrawn and shy boy must join activities. The demand for conformity not only makes it impossible for the aggressive boy to show his real face, but does the same for the withdrawn boy. We can realize how dangerous this repression is, since we know how such emotions erupt when they are kept under a lid for a long time. It also makes diagnosis and prognosis of behavior outside the institution almost impossible.

In working with groups it is important to discover those members who have potentialities for leadership. Among delinquents this is especially important, since the gang leader is a key figure. It is valuable to find the boys who have such possibilities and help them use their talents in a positive rather than a destructive way. In this group RAY apparently had the makings of an indigenous leader. The fact that he could use his power over the group in whatever way he chose indicates how important it is that we learn to recognize such boys and work intensively with them.

What made RAY attractive to his contemporaries? (1) He was physically strong and attractive, but not threatening (2) He had an innate sense of humor, which made him less vulnerable to teasing by the others. (3) He had a calm attitude toward adults, something most delinquents lack but want badly. (4) He had a friendly charm, which he turned toward the boys as well as toward adults. (5) His emotions seemed less complex than those of most of the others; there was some kind of stability about him that impressed the boys.

RAY could have directed the group at will. It was therefore important, for his own sake as well as for the group, that he learn how to use his qualities not as a dictator, but as a participant and leader. In many institutions boys like RAY have been used to police the other boys, capitalizing on their power over the group. This practice will drive the outstanding boy more and more into the gang type of leadership. By helping RAY take an active part in the elections and letting him see his job as an elected one, some beginning was made toward giving him an outlet for his qualities, yet keeping them in the framework of a democratic society. However, continued work with him would certainly be necessary.

The two other boys chosen by the group as the ones who would make the best leaders showed characteristics similar to RAY's. HARRY, who received the greatest number of votes as the boy best suited for leadership, was the only Negro in the whole group. His qualities were also physical strength, a quiet, relaxed attitude toward adults, and a similar quiet in relation to other boys. He usually showed more impartiality in a dispute than did the other boys.

The lack of race prejudice in the group was outstanding. The main reasons for this seemed to be: (1) the fact that the boys felt they were all in the same boat; (2) the genuine non-segregation policy in the center; and (3) the positive qualities of the boy who was the lone representative of the Negro minority.

One goal of the group worker is to help the individual and the group to come to some kind of self-determination. This project showed that even in the short time of one month, progress can be made toward that goal. It was typical that the freedom given in the group was at first viewed with alarm by some of the boys. They could see discipline only in terms of punishment and repression. The records show the gradual change. The idea of self-government appeared and was carried out—or at least a beginning of it—in the elections. The choice of officers throws a pathetic sidelight on the kind of society most of the boys know. In any other club the officers suggested would have been chairman, treasurer, secretary, etc. These boys suggested the offices of mayor, judge, policeman, sheriff, and probation officer. It is also significant that the first reaction of one of the officeholders was that now *he* could punish the others. This shows the danger of self-government for immature youngsters without the help and guidance of an accepting adult. In the course of time the group relied less and less on formal control, and was able to apply some form of self-control. This was demonstrated in the last meetings, when the boys were able to spread out over a comparatively large area without misusing their freedom.

Concerning the Discussion Meetings

The spontaneous participation of the boys in these discussions was outstanding. This was possible only because a friendly relationship had previously been established in the informal meetings. Too often therapeutic discussion groups are only painful quiz sessions or lectures, because such a relationship has not been established. In any therapeutic attempt, whether with a group or with an individual, a positive relationship between the worker and the client or member of the group is essential.

The presence of only one worker seemed to help the informal exchange of thoughts. Observation of other discussion groups indicates that whenever visitors or observers are present, the group members tend either to withdraw or to show off.

The basic group work principle—"Start where the group is"—is as important in the discussion group as in any other activity. It was important to talk a simple language that could be easily understood. It was also necessary to let the boys start with the subjects closest to their interest—school, for instance—not with a lecture on probation or adolescence. The group discussions had to allow for some verbal release of tension and hostility. If the worker becomes moralistic or defensive in regard to himself, the institution, or society, he has already defeated his purpose. Insight and moral values develop slowly, after emotional blocks are moved out of the way. It is significant that the boys were able to see their own part in their difficulties only after they had been allowed free expression of their resentment against what had happened to them.

If a stay in an institution is to have any value for the boys, they must gain some insight not only into the causes of their own behavior, but also into the organizational setup of their surroundings. It was apparently helpful for the newcomers to understand clearly the setup of the Youth Conservation Commission, and for the boys who were about to leave to be prepared for probation.

The group discussions should be directed mainly toward the boys' feelings about themselves and their surroundings. They need a chance to express their guilt, their relationships to their parents and to authority, and their fear of facing the community. The difficulties encountered by a delinquent boy returning to his community have never been enough appreciated. We have a huge literature about the difficulties of the returned soldier, but we have had little to say about the youngsters who come back from institutional life to face a curious, hostile, tempting, and thoroughly bewildering environment.

The worker in such a discussion group must master the discussion method in a group. The best knowledge of individual behavior will be lost if the worker cannot help each person in the group to express his thoughts, if he has not learned to relate the remarks of one participant to those of another, or to pick up casual remarks which are significant but were missed by the others.

The reception centers of the Youth Commission have as their purpose the study and treatment of delinquent children. This study and treatment, together with schooling and training, should be the task of all our institutions for delinquents. We will need personnel that combines a basic warmth and acceptance of the youngsters with a professional knowledge of the specific field. As these records show, the group worker, as one of the team of the institutional staff, will have a contribution to make in direct work with the youngsters. Since it is probable that few institutions can employ trained group workers for all the work with the youngsters, these trained workers will have to lend their knowledge and skill also to the supervision and training of other staff members, selected for their basic positive attitude toward the youngsters and for their flexibility and willingness to learn.

The group worker should also help in establishing a closer relationship between the probation officer and the social group work services offered in the neighborhood of the youngster who has returned to his community. This cooperation will help the youngster to find his way more easily into groups of contemporaries who will accept him, and to find adults who will be willing to listen to him when he needs them. In this way the services of the group worker can become a link between the protected environment in the institution and the demands of the community.

PART II. GROUP MEETINGS WITH ADOLESCENT GIRLS IN A CHILD GUIDANCE CLINIC

The records of one month of work in an institution can indicate only partially the contribution professional social group work can make in helping emotionally upset youngsters. For this reason the records of group meetings with adolescent girls in a child guidance clinic are presented here to show what can be done to help youngsters in their day-by-day adjustment while living in their own homes.

In the child guidance clinic the group worker is one of a team of experts working with children who are emotionally upset. In this setting the youngsters do not live at the clinic but come for weekly individual interviews with the psychiatrist and weekly group meetings with the social group worker. Concurrently, intensive work is done with each child's parents.

This specific group of girls started meeting during the spring, when they met each week for two hours in the afternoon at the clinic itself. During the school vacation in summer they met once a week for a whole day in one of the city parks. The group met over a period of about one year. The records of six of these meetings are presented here. Case histories of the six girls precede the records of the meetings. Summaries of the progress of three of the girls, written by the group worker at the end of the treatment period, are included at the end to help the reader analyze the effectiveness of group work in diagnosis and treatment.

ANN.   12 years.   IQ 100; PQ* 101

Ann, a Negro girl, is the second child in a family of moderate income. She lives with her brother and mother. Reason for referral to the agency: She has a poor attitude toward school and is disobedient. Reason for referral to the group: Ann needs a permissive group, as she is very tense and unable to play. Ann attended the group for one month.

EILEEN.   15 years.   IQ 87; PQ 48

Eileen is the second of two siblings. She lives with her parents and sister. The family has a moderate income. Reason for referral to the agency: Eileen is receiving endocrine treatment, but not responding well. She shows maladjustment in personal and social areas. Reason for referral to group: Eileen needs help in social adjustment and in gaining self-confidence. Eileen attended the group for three months.

ELAINE.   16 years.   IQ 105; PQ 69, 86

Elaine is the second of two children and lives with her mother, nephew, and sister. They are on a marginal income. She was referred to the agency because of nervous symptoms of three years' standing and no school attendance for three years. (Diagnosis: psychoneurosis or schizophrenia; anxiety state, compulsive slowness.) Reason for referral to the group: Elaine needs slow introduction to social contacts and preparation for eventual return to school. The Rorschach test indicated schizophrenic trends at the beginning of treatment, and that Elaine is idealistic, ambitious, and not practical. Elaine attended the group for eleven months.

* PQ is an abbreviation for Performance Quotient.

ELSIE.   12 years.   IQ 88

Elsie is the second of two children of a marginal income family. She lives with her mother and brother. Reason for referral to the agency: She was referred by a juvenile court for stealing and running away. Elsie also has conflicts with her mother and brother. Reason for referral to the group: Elsie needs companionship, since she is rejected by her neighborhood as a delinquent. Also, diagnostic material is needed to understand her needs better. The Rorschach test showed her to be greatly disturbed, with oppositional and schizoid tendencies. Elsie attended the group for three months.

THELMA.   15 years.   IQ 85; PQ 65

Thelma, a Negro girl, is the oldest of three children. She lives with her parents and sisters on a moderate income. Reason for referral to the agency: She exhibited strange behavior, such as crying, grinning, enuresis, and physical symptoms. Reason for referral to the group: Thelma is rejected by her mother and needs recreational outlets in a small group. The Rorschach test indicated depressive tendencies and ambition. Thelma was in the group for nine months.

VIRGINIA.   13 years.   IQ 100; PQ 95

Virginia, a Negro girl, is an only child, living with her parents and her son, aged two. The family income is marginal. Reason for referral to the agency: Virginia has been oversized all her life, had a child when she was eleven, and is now beginning to steal. Reason for referral to the group: At a court hearing she asked for a chance. She has been changed to another school, intensive treatment is planned, and referral to a group is part of that treatment. She needs an accepting environment. The Rorschach test showed her to be sensitive and ambitious. Virginia attended the group for ten months.

RECORDS OF SIX MEETINGS

First Meeting

When W entered the room EILEEN, ELAINE, and ANN were present. W said hello, and all three girls answered politely but shyly. ELAINE is a tall, blond, lovely girl. She wore a pale blue dress with red buttons and some blue violets pinned on her shoulder. This tended to emphasize her softness. She had a sad expression on her face but tried to smile when she saw W. ANN is a slim, pretty, colored girl with a soft reddish glow in her cheeks. She smiled self-consciously whenever W turned toward her. EILEEN appears to be rather clumsy and is almost as tall as ELAINE.

The three girls went up to W's office. The chairs were arranged in a semicircle so that they could sit together, but almost unconsciously the girls pushed their chairs back so that they formed a row facing W. W began by saying she was glad they had all come. She explained that this would be a small club in which they wanted to become good friends. She said it wouldn't be easy to be friends, since they were all strangers and even came from different neighborhoods, but by coming to meetings they could learn to know each other. W explained further that the club would remain small and that they would have the right to decide what they would like to do—handicrafts, playing outside, making things in the workshop, or maybe taking trips around the city. W asked several times what they would like to do, but for some ten minutes the girls' only response was nodding or slight facial expressions. W felt they might like to work on some materials she had brought and proceeded to find some colored beads for making bracelets. When she showed them a bracelet she had made, the first response came from EILEEN, who said the bracelet was just lovely. ELAINE nodded seriously and said she liked that.

96

It was interesting to observe how the first contact began. While W turned to the cupboard, EILEEN asked ELAINE how old she was. ELAINE gave her age, then EILEEN, and finally ANN. It was EILEEN who started the spark of interaction between the girls. ANN seemed almost as withdrawn as ELAINE, with little expression on her face. Since they seemed interested in the beads, W asked ELAINE what color she would like to work with. Her first spontaneous response was "pale blue." She said she'd like to mix it with another color but didn't know which one. W suggested red, because there were red buttons on her dress. ELAINE smiled as if pleased when W commented on her violets. She looked up in a shy manner, saying, "Oh, thank you for liking them and thinking they are pretty." EILEEN chose more easily than the other two, taking all brown. ANN first said black, then asked to mix red with black.

At this point W was called downstairs to greet a new arrival. W told the girls she would meet a new girl and bring her back. W felt this was a good opportunity to leave the girls alone, without the presence of an adult. The moment she left the room she heard EILEEN begin talking, then more voices, and soon all three were discussing their ages and schools. W didn't hear ELAINE's response to the girls' questions about school, but later on during the meeting ELAINE mentioned three times that she had not been in school for quite a while and would like to go back soon.

W met ELSIE in the waiting room. She was a vivacious, short girl with lively brown eyes which seemed to dance in her very expressive face. She was dressed like a typical high school girl in a dark brown sweater, a snow-white collar, and saddle shoes. W greeted her in a friendly fashion and felt that ELSIE was hesitant, but also friendly. As she went upstairs with W, she said that she had to go to the washroom first. After she was through, she and W went upstairs, and on the way W told her a little about the club, mentioning that the other girls had already arrived.

Elsie was greeted in a friendly way, and W knew that during the time she had been downstairs the girls had talked to each other. Elsie at once got very interested in the beads and was very sure what colors she wanted. Since Elsie wanted some red beads too, W seated her beside Elaine, and that way the girls shared the beads. While working and moving their hands they became more at ease. Ann was working fastest and finished her bracelet very quickly. The others took a little longer time with the work. Nevertheless, there was no outstanding slowness on Elaine's part, nor any special inability to cope with this task on the part of Eileen. The beadwork was very simple to do, but when it was finished it looked so nice that it seemed like much more expert work than it actually was, and definitely gave the girls great satisfaction.

While they were working, W got out some candy and asked the girls if they wanted some. Eileen shook her head and said she couldn't because it was Pessach. The other three said they weren't eating candy because it was Lent. W said she thought they were really fine to be able to stick to their vows. She put the candy away, saying they would have it at other meetings. Again there were a few minutes of silence, but W felt it would be easier now to get some conversation going. She asked them whether they would like to go on some trips. Eileen knew the city a little better than the others and had visited the university. The others said they would like to go, and that they also liked the out-of-doors.

W asked whether they had been at any camps. Ann got a little more lively at this point. She said she had been at Camp C. and loved it, and that she hopes to go there this year for at least six weeks. Elsie said she wasn't so sure she would be allowed to go. She said this with a half-smile, and the expression on her face indicated pretty clearly to W that Elsie wondered whether W thought she should have such freedom. W said that maybe it could be arranged anyway, and that W thought camp was swell. Eileen had been at Camp E., and both she and Ann were very happy that W

knew their camps. ELAINE shook her head and said that she
hadn't been at any camp, but that she might like to see one.
Again ELAINE spoke with some hesitance, but without exaggerated slowness.

W asked the girls what they would like best to do in their
club. After some moments of silence W said it might be a
good idea to make the rounds and just ask everybody what
they most liked to do. ANN started out and became more
lively as she said that she liked best to sing or to study history.
This brought a response from ELAINE, who said that she was
most interested in ancient history, especially Egyptian history,
and that she also loved music. ANN said she played the cello
and the violin. W said well, that was swell, and maybe she
could bring her violin to the group. ANN said, "Yes, ma'am,"
but her expression clearly said that she didn't want to bring
it. W laughed and said she thought ANN really would like to
say no, that she mightn't want to bring her violin. ANN smiled
and said she really didn't want to bring the violin, and didn't
like to play it because she didn't think she played it well.
W said this was not a place where you had to say yes to every
suggestion, that they had the freedom to say no whenever
they felt like it. W caught a glance from ELSIE and a big smile.

EILEEN said she liked singing most. She liked literature and
listening to records too. ANN added then that she would like
to do some painting, and W mentioned the workshop. ELAINE
mentioned fingerpainting, after W spoke of it, and said that
would be something she would like to do. W told them about
the possibility of combining fingerpainting with music, and
they got very excited and interested in the idea. At this point
W felt there was a real conversation going, not just each one
telling what she wanted. Interestingly enough, it was ELAINE
who picked up the interests of the others and added her own.
When it was ELAINE's turn she had to repeat practically everything she had said—her interest in ancient history, painting,
music, and going on trips. ELSIE said she liked painting too,
and drawing and playing ball. While they were talking about

all this, most of the girls had finished their bracelets and W fitted them to their arms. They all wore them and thought they were beautiful.

The girls asked W whether she had a ball, and ELAINE said in quite a lively manner that she would love to play. W suggested going downstairs to the workshop to look at it and see whether they would prefer to meet there instead of in her office. Afterward, she said, we might go out and play ball, since it was such a nice day. The girls left their wraps in W's office and were much more lively going downstairs than they had been coming up.

In the workshop ELSIE was almost dancing up and down the aisle. They all decided they would rather meet there than upstairs. They got out the ball, which ELSIE quickly grabbed, and went over to an empty lot. The girls looked around and said that this was really not so bad. They were surprised that the clinic had such a good place to play. W laughed and said she didn't think it was so good, but anyway it was better than nothing. The girls quickly decided on a game of volleyball, and ELAINE and EILEEN, the ones who knew the game best, explained it to the others. ELAINE said, "I just love to play ball." ELAINE and ELSIE were on one side, and EILEEN and ANN on the other.

While the girls were playing ball, W kept score. The girls played in a very harmonious way and definitely enjoyed it. EILEEN and ANN generally lost to ELAINE and ELSIE, though very often the scores were pretty close. After four or six games had been played, they decided to make a large circle and just throw and catch the ball.

When it was time to leave, it was again ELSIE who took the ball. While going upstairs ELAINE said, "This is the first time in three years that I've played ball and I like it." While they were putting on their coats they started for the first time to look around W's room and at the pictures. ELSIE was especially interested in a picture of some Japanese girls. She thought they looked beautiful. ELAINE said she had started a scrapbook of movie stars, and maybe they could start scrapbooks here too. ELSIE and ANN stood before a map entitled, "The Nation, One People from Many Countries." They said they had seen a map like that before and they liked it. EILEEN and ELAINE stood together and smiled at the crude designs of some younger children that W had pinned up in her room. They asked W how old the kids were who had made those designs.

The girls discovered that they all had to walk to the street-car, so they walked together. EILEEN asked W whether she could lend her a nickel; she would give W a car-check for it be-cause she had promised her mother to telephone and had forgotten. W gave her the nickel and said she should keep the car-check in case she should need it. EILEEN then left to make her telephone call. The other three and W walked to the car stop together. ELAINE said then that she would walk over to M. Hospital where her mother works. She was a little hesitant at first about the right direction, but when it was pointed out to her she knew where to go. She smiled when she left, saying that she really had enjoyed the meeting. She hadn't known that she was coming to a group—she had thought she had an appointment with the psychiatrist. W said to her, "Well, I'm sorry, I hope you weren't too disappointed." ELAINE smiled even more, shook her head, and said she had really liked it. She left then, and W watched her walking rather slowly and hesitantly along the street.

ELSIE and ANN got on the same streetcar as W. There were two seats, and ELSIE quickly urged the others to sit down, saying, "Boy, I'd much rather stand than sit." W laughed and said that ELSIE looked like somebody who liked to do a lot of jumping around. ELSIE laughed too. ANN for the first time started to talk continuously, talking again about camp. ELSIE asked ANN whether the girls in camp slept in beds or on cots. Apparently she didn't like cots. ANN assured her that they slept in beds. W told ELSIE that she looked like a good camper, like somebody who would love the out-of-doors. ELSIE said that she might, but she just wasn't sure whether she'd ever really go to a camp. She talked about having joined the Girl Scouts, however.

Somehow the subject of songs and singing came up, and W said that maybe some of the girls could sing songs in different languages. ELSIE said, "Oh yes, I can sing in Hungarian—oh, no, I mean Latin, like in church." It was interesting that she apparently wanted to avoid talking about being Hungarian. When ELSIE left the streetcar she stood on the other side of the street and waved to us until the car had passed. The rest of the way W rode with ANN, who talked a little about her interest in history. She said everything in a shy, hesitant way, but W felt that a little contact had been established.

Second Meeting

EILEEN and ELAINE were the first ones to arrive, and W took them down to the workshop. They were much freer than the first time, and it was clear that they felt they knew W and the environment. EILEEN immediately pulled out her report card and asked if W was interested in seeing it. W certainly was and was surprised to see that she had all S's and two A's. W said it was certainly a very good report card. ELAINE seemed very interested too, and almost envious.

EILEEN talked quickly and freely. She said she had had to miss school the day the report cards were given out, and she had been terribly worried—frightened to death about what had happened—so she was very happy when she discovered that the report card really was not bad. She then said this might be the last time she could come to the group because the principal did not want to give her any more time off. She showed W the note her mother had written, and the principal had marked it, "O.K., but only for today." EILEEN said she certainly had to be out of school an awful lot, because she had to go to the hospital and so on, but she wished she could come. W said that she would talk this over with the case worker and the psychiatrist, and that they could probably manage to get her to the group. W had heard that when

EILEEN got home from the first meeting she had said, "This was the most beautiful day of my life."

W had prepared starch for fingerpainting. ELAINE looked at it a little doubtfully and said she had never done anything like that. Both girls were interested in the victrola, however. W told them there were lots of records, and they got very enthusiastic over the records as they took them out. They put them all on the table and chose music to put on, always finding more and more that they wanted to play. At one point W said again that the girls needn't say yes all the time. Later, when W asked whether they wanted to do some painting while they listened, ELAINE looked straight at W with a knowing smile and said, "Well, I'm just looking now at the records; I wouldn't like to do any painting." W laughed, and ELAINE joined her when W said, "Well, you certainly learned to say no."

It struck W all through the meeting how much ELAINE was conscious of her sickness—of being slow, and unable to make contact with others—and of every step toward recovery that she was able to make. The girls were listening to Tannhäuser first, and both ELAINE and EILEEN said they wished they could go to an opera someday. They had never seen one, but they had listened to the records and they certainly would like to. W said that maybe they could go together. They then put on the Hungarian Rhapsody.

At that point ELSIE came downstairs looking very lovely and tomboyish in light blue slacks, with her hair flying. She came in and sat on a chair, listening to the music. ELAINE said she just loved the Hungarian Rhapsody. W said she liked Hungarian music because it had so much rhythm. ELSIE said that her parents came from Hungary. This was the first time, apparently, that she felt she could talk about her origin. W asked her whether she knew the language, and she said that she knew only a few words. ELAINE rather hesitantly said that her parents had come from Germany, and that she knew more than a few words of German. W said that she could speak it too, and maybe someday they could speak all different kinds of languages.

W talked about the opera, and W told the girls that there would be a wonderful concert on Sunday and maybe she could get tickets. EILEEN said she didn't think she could come, and ELSIE smiled and said it would be impossible, since she had a date. She then pulled out a piece of paper, put it before W, and said that W should look at it. It was a beautifully drawn bat with a human face, and ELSIE explained that this was the Batman. All around the paper were written such questions as, "Do you want to go out with me tomorrow?" and "Will you kiss me in the dark?" W gave it back to ELSIE, saying she thought it was beautifully designed and lovely handwriting. ELSIE laughed and looked at W as if she wanted to say, "Well, that's not what I gave it to you for." Then she said, "Well, don't you think it's bad?" W said no, she didn't think so, and besides, it often happens that people want you to go out with them or ask you whether you love them. ELSIE answered, "Well, you didn't see what he said in the corner of the paper." W said he had said something about kissing her in the dark, but W knew that boys and girls liked to kiss each other.

ELAINE and EILEEN were present at this conversation, but it seemed to be alien to them, and they didn't enter it at all. ELSIE said this boy friend of hers came to see her on Sunday afternoons, and she could go out with him until evening but she had to be home in the evening. She had had another boy friend too, but she had changed, and now the other one was jealous. She seemed to enjoy all the attention she got from the boys.

W got out the candy and EILEEN and ELSIE ate a little, but ELAINE took almost nothing. W asked her whether she didn't like it. She shook her head, smiled her pretty smile, and said what she really liked were pickles, not sweets. ELSIE laughed and said she just loved candy and was only being polite in not taking too much. W said she certainly could eat the candy if she liked it.

W asked whether they would like to go out to play ball. ELSIE jumped up like a little colt, smiled, and said sure, that's what she wanted. The others also wanted to, so they took the volleyball, a baseball bat, a softball, and the candy and went out. When the door opened, ELSIE cried, "Ahh, air." W laughed and asked her if she felt terribly cooped up. She said yes, everything was too closed in; she loved to be outside and moving around. She also drew W's attention to her wearing slacks, saying they were not allowed to do this in school but she just loved to wear them. All this behavior indicated clearly that she needed a lot of freedom and that all restrictions were very hard on her.

The girls had a wonderful time playing ball. W was amazed at how they had loosened up. EILEEN had brought back the nickel W had lent her last time, and W put it in the candy box, which they left near a tree so that it would be safe. ELAINE laughed and put a car-check in the box, saying that it would be safe too. It was these little things that made W feel the girls had become much more outgoing. There was a lot of laughter all during the game, which was played quite intently by both sides. This time W participated in the game. ELSIE had a great knack for throwing the ball very far, and W kidded her, saying she was really "mean." Sometimes when the others won some points, ELSIE turned to W, who was her partner, and said, "Well, I think I have to be mean again, don't I?" It was all done with a lot of good humor. Frequently, when the ball fell far out in the street, some passing man would pick it up and throw it back. The girls were quite amused about these polite men, and again it was ELSIE who summed up the situation. She said that now she would always watch and throw her farthest balls when a man was passing, because that way we would save a lot of energy. All three girls did a lot of running after the ball, especially ELAINE. She was sometimes quite amused and said she soon would have to lie down and go to bed, but she certainly would not stop. W once suggested a rest up on the hill, but they just went on playing.

Later the girls took the bat and the softball, and W was

amazed to see how well ELAINE could hit. She and ELSIE were
really good ball players. EILEEN was the last one to get a
chance to bat, and it was almost impossible for her to hit the
ball. W was impressed by the patience both ELSIE and ELAINE
showed toward EILEEN. They threw the ball to her again and
again, maybe forty or fifty times, so that she could have her
try at hitting the ball. They were never laughing at her. This
was probably the first occasion on which EILEEN was able to
try something like this without others getting impatient with
her. She finally hit the ball once, and this was quite an accomplishment.

Once during the game ELSIE laughed at W and said, "You
know, I'm man crazy." W said, "All men?" That stopped her
for a moment, then she said, "No, really not all of them, just
good-looking ones." W said, "Well, that shows some discrimination, doesn't it?"

It was time to leave, and the girls got their things. ELAINE
helped W bring the balls upstairs, and W asked her whether
she was very tired. She said, "No, I'm not as tired as I have
been. I feel much better than in a long time."

Third Meeting

When W came into the waiting room ANN and VIRGINIA
had arrived. VIRGINIA was new in the group. She is a tall, dark-
skinned colored girl with very attractive features and lively
dark eyes. She looks much older than her almost thirteen
years. Both she and ANN were a little hesitant, since ANN had
not been at the last meeting. W told her the group had
missed her, but she was rather silent. Downstairs W showed
VIRGINIA the workshop, saying that it was a rather primitive
place, but that the girls had decided they would like to meet
here first and go outside whenever they wanted to play outdoors. W had bought a cake and candles for ELSIE's birthday,
and she suggested that ANN and VIRGINIA help fix the cake.
This activity brought the two girls more together. They asked
how old ELSIE would be. W said thirteen, so they put in

thirteen candles and one for good luck. ANN held the cake and VIRGINIA put the candles in.

ANN asked VIRGINIA how old she was, and VIRGINIA said twelve, with a rather unhappy expression on her face. ANN said in an almost admiring way, "Well, you certainly have grown fast." VIRGINIA shrugged her shoulders, and W said it was sometimes tough to be so tall early in life, because people always expected you to act so grown-up. W had not really expected such a change in VIRGINIA's face and her whole behavior. She suddenly looked up, smiled at W, nodded her head vehemently, and said with great conviction, "That's it. They think you should act grown-up." After this she was able to talk in a more lively fashion.

We heard some footsteps outside and ANN said eagerly, "If it's ELSIE, I'll stall her so she can't see the cake." It was ELSIE, and ANN very skillfully diverted her upstairs. W is fairly sure, however, that ELSIE suspected something. A few minutes later ELAINE came down too. She wore her hair hanging loose on her shoulders and W thinks it was a little curled at the ends. VIRGINIA told her about the birthday cake, and they took it to the back of the workshop, where they built a kind of wall in front of it. W had matches and asked ELAINE to light the candles. It was interesting to observe her doing this. She did it hesitantly, as if she was a little afraid, but she managed quite well because nobody hurried her.

When ANN and ELSIE came in, ELSIE smiled and said she thought she knew what was coming. W asked ELSIE how her speech had gone in school. She said it had gone fine—that she had made two or three mistakes but she didn't think it had been too bad. She looked very pretty in a red skirt and a white blouse with red embroidery. She said she had wanted to look real clean, and therefore she had gone home at noon to change to this outfit. She was proud and very pleased with her accomplishment in school.

W introduced VIRGINIA to all of them, and the girls nodded to each other in a very friendly way. ELSIE and ELAINE were thinking of EILEEN and said they weren't sure she would come. Last time she had said she might not be able to. W told them that she had called EILEEN's school and she thought it would be possible for EILEEN to come. W thought it was quite an indication of a developing awareness of each other that the two girls mentioned EILEEN and also remembered what she had said last time.

Just then EILEEN came downstairs. She had one hand in a bandage. W had heard previously that she had sprained her wrist playing ball at the last meeting. When W asked her how she was, she laughed and said it wasn't bad, that the bandage would come off the next day. By this time ELAINE had lighted all the candles on the cake. The lights in the workshop were turned off and ELAINE brought out the cake. Everybody sang "Happy Birthday" to ELSIE. She smiled and looked really happy. W put her ring on the candle in the middle and said that everybody should make a wish. ELSIE smiled even more, and when she blew out the candles with one breath her feat was greeted quite jubilantly by the others.

W asked if ELSIE wanted to tell them what she had wished for. She started to, then looked around, and said with a smile, "No, there are too many around." EILEEN answered to this, "Well, how is your boy friend, ELSIE?" Then ELSIE said in a surprised voice, "Now, how did she know? It was him I was thinking of when I made the wish." Even ELAINE smiled.

The girls sat around the table and looked very happy and gay. ELSIE was cutting the cake. She had counted how many were present and divided the cake so that everybody had a really large piece with candles sticking in it. The girls laughed and said they wouldn't be able to eat any supper after this. ELSIE and ELAINE got the biggest pieces and ELAINE looked rather embarrassed. W kidded her a little, saying that she had thought of bringing the pickles ELAINE liked, but that they didn't quite fit for a birthday. ELAINE took this very well, laughed, and said she would try to eat this big piece of cake anyhow. While eating, there was quite a lively conversation. EILEEN talked a lot about school. ELSIE said that in her school they were selling tickets for a concert and she wished they all could go together.

During all this time ELAINE had kept on her very light coat. EILEEN and ELSIE asked her if she wasn't hot, but she said she wasn't and kept the coat on. Even later, during the ball game, she kept it on until she got really hot, and then she hesitated to take it off, asking where she could put it so it wouldn't get dirty. W then held the coat for her. W felt that ELAINE showed quite a bit of anxiety about getting the coat dirty. (One of ELAINE's symptoms was compulsive hand-washing.)

While the girls were sitting around the table, W asked them whether they wanted to do something in the workshop or go out and play ball. It was amusing to see how difficult it was for them to make the decision, since they weren't sure what W wanted. W smiled and encouraged each one to say which she really preferred. ANN was the first one to speak up. She said she'd like to go out. After that they loosened up and each one said she wanted to go outdoors.

W felt that ELSIE was too well-dressed to play ball and suggested that she put on a smock that was hanging downstairs. When she had put it on, everybody laughed because it was much too long for her. W exchanged her own shorter smock for this one, and ELSIE looked really pretty in W's smock. She said she wished she could take it away from W because it looked so nice on her.

The girls played volleyball, Indian ball, and finally baseball. It is difficult to describe the happiness and feeling of relaxation that were present all during this period. There was much laughter, as there had been the last time, and a real feeling of enjoyment. There was very little competitive spirit. The girls simply enjoyed the game. They were glad to have VIRGINIA with them since she was the same size as ELAINE, and the two could match each other on opposite sides. ELSIE told VIRGINIA proudly about the polite men who had caught the balls on the hill, and said she hoped there would be some men passing again today.

ELAINE did a lot of running again and got very hot. ELSIE said she wondered whether ELAINE would get completely exhausted again. W asked ELAINE if it was too much for her, but she shook her head and said, "You know, exercise can't really hurt anybody. I'm glad I can do it." ANN entered the game surprisingly well. She ran and shouted and got much satisfaction out of it. EILEEN continually hit the ball with her injured hand, although everybody shouted at her not to do it. She laughed and said there was really nothing much wrong with her hand. It seemed to mean a lot to her that she could use this hand.

When it came to playing with the ball and bat, however, EILEEN withdrew and said she couldn't do that so well. She sat down on the grass and watched the others. Soon W joined her, saying to the others that she was a little tired too. While W was sitting beside her, EILEEN told W how much she liked the other girls and how much she liked to play these games. W observed the other four girls, and each one enjoyed every part of the game.

When it was time to leave, VIRGINIA and ELSIE went up together to return W's balls to her office. They stayed quite a while in the washroom. ELAINE, ANN, EILEEN, and W went downstairs to the workshop to get their coats. ELAINE said she hoped they could always have one period to play at their meetings, and ANN nodded. EILEEN said she had again forgotten to bring money with her, this time to get something for her mother. W loaned her the money, since she had brought it back very punctually the last time.

All five girls stood in the waiting room finally, talking together and planning what they would do next time. VIRGINIA's mother, a very pleasant-looking young woman, stood nearby and smiled happily. As they left, VIRGINIA asked ANN which way she went, and said, "What a pity. I wish you and I were going the same way." This suggested that some kind of relationship had already sprung up between the two girls. W walked to the streetcar with VIRGINIA and her mother. VIRGINIA's mother smiled and said she thought the girls had had

a really wonderful time. VIRGINIA said she had certainly had a
wonderful time, that ELSIE had told her she was going to wear
slacks next time, and that she would like to wear slacks too.
She waved happily when she left.

Eleventh Meeting

[The group had continued to meet, and the girls had gone
on several trips, learning to know the city and each other.
ELAINE, especially, had made progress in relating to others
and in moving more freely and quickly. ELSIE had been found
by the police staying out late at night, and—since this meant
a breaking of probation—she was sent to a training school.
This unfortunately interrupted work with her at the clinic.
During the summer the clinic's group program changed into
full-day meetings once a week in the city park. ANN left for
camp during this period, and later her mother felt that treatment was no longer necessary. EILEEN went to camp for two
weeks, but later joined the group again for a short period. A
new fifteen-year-old girl, THELMA, who did not respond to
individual treatment, joined the group during the summer
months.]

A picnic had been planned for this meeting, but it turned
out to be a very dark and rainy day. W was waiting for the
girls, and quite late, about fifty minutes after the usual meeting time, VIRGINIA and a cousin of hers named Shirley arrived.
VIRGINIA had brought some records and books and a big
lunch box, and she was very disappointed when she saw that
nobody else had arrived. She said her mother had packed the
lunch box so that she could give everybody some, and she
hoped at least one or two of the girls would come. W said
that she was disappointed too, but that the rain probably had
kept some of the girls away.

After a little while VIRGINIA said in her good-natured way,
"Well, we'll have fun anyway." She did not mention the
incident of the week before and W did not press the issue.
[Last week VIRGINIA had told her mother that the group
planned to go horseback riding. Her mother had given her

money, and Virginia had left as if for the group meeting. Instead, she had spent the day by herself at the movies.] After a time Virginia asked W to call and find out if the other girls were coming. She said that she had missed Elaine—she hadn't seen her since spring. W tried to call Elaine, but there was no way to reach her. W then called Thelma. Her sister said that Thelma had left a long time ago.

Thelma came quite a while later, and everyone pretended to shake her fists at her as she arrived. Thelma smiled and said, "Don't be angry at me; I have no excuse, I'm just late." She wore a very pretty blouse, and Virginia and W both mentioned it. Virginia introduced Thelma to Shirley, and Thelma said she had heard about this cousin, the one whose mother always wore those elegant clothes. This remark showed how much talk about each other there is in the neighborhood. Virginia was much happier now and said it was swell—this way we had four girls. Thelma said she had invited another girl, and although she couldn't come, Thelma could have invited one or two more. Virginia said she would miss "my friend Elsie." W told her it was true that Elsie wasn't coming back, and Virginia accepted the fact.

While walking to the picnic spot W and the girls discussed some of the future plans for the group. W told the girls she could get a car to take them on an excursion into town. They were very enthusiastic about this idea, but Thelma said that next week she couldn't come because she was going to a picnic with her Sunday school. It had been planned a long time ago. W said she would try to arrange the trip so that Thelma could be present, since she had been very regular about coming to the group. The girls all expressed some anger that Elaine and Eileen had not come today. W said it was a disappointment when somebody let us down. Virginia nodded silently, and W thinks she understood very well that she had done the same thing last time.

When the group reached the picnic place W started to hand out knives and told the girls to cut sticks for roasting the wieners. Thelma exclaimed, "Oh, this is fun! This is like a real picnic." They wanted to have paper plates and cups, so THELMA and VIRGINIA said they would go over to the cabin to get them. They were quite proud of taking the keys and going off by themselves. Meanwhile W prepared some of the food with Shirley. When the girls came back they also brought the victrola. They wanted to hear the records, and they enjoyed the wild sound of the music. VIRGINIA asked THELMA to dance, but when THELMA shook her head and said she didn't know how, VIRGINIA danced with her cousin. THELMA looked at W and said, "I really know how to dance. I just didn't know whether it was right." W said, why, certainly it was all right, and if she wanted to, she could show W how to dance.

Just then VIRGINIA and Shirley became so interested in the wiener roast that they stopped dancing. W built the fire, and Shirley, and later VIRGINIA, used the matches to light it. THELMA kept a little in the background. They were all excited about roasting their wieners on the sticks. THELMA was a little clumsy and became terribly embarrassed when she dropped one of the wieners into the fire. Nothing was made of the incident, however, and the wiener was got out with some twigs. THELMA seemed to be happy about this. The girls had brought soft drinks with them and W had brought cookies, so everybody shared everything.

While they were eating, THELMA talked about cooking. She said she liked to fix her lunch or dinner according to colors. She likes to make nice salads too, but her mother said, "Oh, you're not in school, you don't need to do that." THELMA thought that they learned to do things very well in school and that her mother should not interfere. She said her mother's cooking was too starchy, anyway. Her mother also gets annoyed with her when she starts measuring things, but THELMA thought that the way she learned in school made recipes come out well. W said that maybe after she had cooked a lot she wouldn't need to measure any more. THELMA said that was true, but that her mother didn't need to interfere. These remarks were another attempt of THELMA's to express her resentment against the way her mother handles things on every occasion.

VIRGINIA and THELMA got into quite a discussion of cooking, and W could see that they both enjoyed the cooking classes in school. The girls also had a lot of fun toasting marshmallows. What with pop, cookies, marshmallows, a lot of wieners, and the pie that VIRGINIA had brought with her, we all felt quite stuffed. Everybody was tired and sat around on logs, just resting and sometimes singing a little. THELMA brought out a letter she had got from one of her boy friends overseas. She showed the girls a picture he had sent of a ruined town. She said he was a boy from the South, and that she didn't know him but had just started writing to him. She added that he knew how old she was, but she didn't know exactly how old he was.

When we had rested for a while the girls decided that they would go to the cabin and bring back some books and pictures. About now, however, it started to rain, and VIRGINIA asked if they couldn't go to a movie. W said they could, but it turned out that nobody had enough money. VIRGINIA accepted this disappointment very well. After W and the girls had cleaned everything up they went into the cabin. W had brought some books with her, among them some material from the YWCA. The girls were very interested in this since it contained many pictures, and VIRGINIA knew a lot of people in the pictures. THELMA knew a few too. Among them was a woman from the juvenile court, and VIRGINIA said that she had seen her there. This led to a long discussion which was carried mainly by THELMA. THELMA was using these meetings very well to solve her problems. W will try to summarize as completely as possible what was brought out in the next fifteen minutes.

THELMA asked first whether the child guidance clinic was a juvenile court. When W said it wasn't, THELMA wondered what it could be. She said her mother had given her the idea that it was just like the court. W gave THELMA an interpretation of the function of the clinic. In quite a rush of words

THELMA then said that when she had her spells her mother
got so worried that she phoned everywhere. THELMA could
hear her mother telephoning a lot of doctors, and her mother
had noted down a lot of telephone numbers and had seemed
to be terribly frightened. That made THELMA terribly frightened too, especially when she heard her mother call the psychiatric hospital. [THELMA had great difficulty in saying this
word and got mixed up every time. VIRGINIA helped her by
pronouncing each syllable and teaching her to say it right.]
THELMA went on to say that her mother had said somebody
at the clinic would look into her head and tell what was going
on. She looked at W questioningly and asked if this was true,
if somebody really could look into her head? W explained
that this wasn't possible, but that by talking to her people
might find out what was bothering her and be able to help her.

THELMA then said that the first time she came to the clinic
she was almost out of her mind with fear about what would
happen to her. She was sure the psychiatrist must have thought
she was a very disagreeable person, because she was angry and
hurt and afraid and she didn't want to talk to him. She said
she was terribly on her guard not to say anything wrong, because she always thought that maybe they wanted to find out
something about her; but what could it be? She added that if
only she had known it wasn't that bad, she might have acted
differently, but she was just so afraid. She then asked, "But
what is the matter with me? What do you do at the clinic?
Why did you come here, VIRGINIA? What was the matter
with ELAINE, and what does it mean to have St. Vitus' dance?"
[ELAINE had told THELMA at the previous meeting that she
had had St. Vitus' dance. This was how ELAINE identified
her nervous symptoms. Actually, however, she had not had
St. Vitus' dance, and no organic basis for her symptoms had
been discovered.]

W first gave THELMA some understanding and interpretation of what the clinic was trying to do. Since THELMA also
insisted on knowing about the mental hospital, W explained
that there were many people who went there just as to any

other out-patient department of a clinic, and that they could recover just like other sick people. When W started to explain some of the procedures of the child guidance clinic, THELMA said, "My mother said she wouldn't let me come here if she didn't think it would help me. But I don't want to come if she doesn't want me to come." W asked her if she didn't want to come. THELMA suddenly became less angry and said, "Yes, I want to, but I don't want to if my mother hates to have me do it." W told her that her mother probably didn't hate to let her come to the clinic, and that her mother came to the clinic too, to get help in working out all those problems. THELMA said that the lady to whom her mother talks at the clinic must think she, THELMA, is terribly bad, because her mother says that she talks all the time about how THELMA acts. W said that they mainly talked about how THELMA and her mother could get along together, and how her mother could be helped to understand THELMA better.

THELMA asked again what St. Vitus' dance was and what ELAINE had. W explained something about the involuntary movements that people make when they have St. Vitus' dance. She added that it is not always a serious sickness and that people who have it can be helped. THELMA again questioned VIRGINIA, apparently anxious to know why others came to the clinic. VIRGINIA said, "You see, I was very unhappy when I came to the clinic. My father and my mother didn't get along; they were always fighting. My father was so mean and my mother didn't let me go anywhere." THELMA interrupted, "Just the same as mine." Then VIRGINIA said, "Well, we got together when we got things clear and now I'm much happier. Also, my mother and father get along better and my mother lets me go out." She added that she too had been very afraid when she came to the clinic in the beginning.

At this point the discussion was interrupted by Shirley, who called out that the sun had come out. With some relief the two girls ended the conversation and eagerly gathered things together preparatory to going out. W felt that it was quite a good time to be interrupted, since both girls had talked out a lot of their feelings and now needed relief. After this the girls released a lot of their tension by shouting, imitating animals, and acting like two little children—not like the serious youngsters they had been just before.

Later, when they felt tired and wanted to rest, the girls lay on the grass and did a lot of singing. THELMA became quite impatient at times, saying, "People mess up a song." When there was a pause in the singing, THELMA sighed and said that nobody really liked her very much. VIRGINIA with a warm gesture took her in her arms and said, "Well, now, honey, I do." THELMA leaned close to her and they rested in this embrace until THELMA laughed and said, "Well, now she pretends to be my husband." Then she went on, "Oh gosh, I wish I were on my honeymoon." W asked whether she couldn't wait just a little, and THELMA replied, "Five years, that certainly would be too long." VIRGINIA said, "Oh, you know I hate men, but I wish some boys were here." They all laughed, and THELMA said, "Same here. I don't like them and yet I want them." Soon afterward dark clouds came up again, and it was time to leave. The first drops began to fall as they were walking to the streetcar, and W urged the girls to hurry home.

Twelfth Meeting

THELMA had told us the previous time that she would not be able to attend because she was going to a church picnic. W had telephoned earlier to let VIRGINIA know that we would go today to see a planetarium. She was quite pleased about this and said that she would come. W had also left a note for ELAINE, and she said that she too would come.

ELAINE arrived very punctually. She had just come from a test with the psychologist, and W thought she would talk about this. Instead, she suddenly looked quite seriously at W and said she had felt terrible last week and also today, because so often she couldn't sleep at night. Last night it was very bad again. W wondered what the cause was, and for the first time ELAINE let her feelings burst out. All during the rest of the day W felt for the first time that ELAINE was coming closer to other people. ELAINE said, "I can't sleep because my sister fights so much with me. I don't know why she has to hate me so. She was always very mean to me but it's worse now. She nags me all day whenever she can. She says I'm dumb, too dumb to go to school, so why should I go to school now. Formerly she slapped me a lot but now I simply slap back."

W: Do you think you are too dumb to go to school?

ELAINE: No, I really don't think so. I don't know how I made out on the test, but the psychologist told me she would tell you. But I don't think I'm so dumb and I want to learn. It's funny, I had to be sick and I'm the one who wants to learn, and she doesn't like learning and she went to school.

W: Did she finish school?

ELAINE: Yes, she did finish school, but she never liked it. She is just not interested in those things. She likes to jitterbug and go out dancing, while I like ancient history and things like that. It's crazy.

W: Do you think it is crazy?

ELAINE: No, I don't think so. I really like it, and when we went into the museum you showed me a lot about it. And I even went up one day and asked somebody in the library, and they gave me art books on it. I just like it. Well, I don't know, I think maybe she is jealous of me. I think she is jealous that I am healthy now and can go back to school. Why should she be that way?

W: Well, now think; for such a long time you could be her baby, and now she has to let you go. Maybe that makes her angry.

ELAINE: (Quite excited) That sure is it. I sure was her baby. She could do with me whatever she wanted to and she did, and now she can't and it makes her mad.

It was amazing how easily ELAINE could understand the situation the moment she started to talk about it. W said to her that her sister probably wasn't so happy either. Then

ELAINE said, "She certainly isn't. She used to work, but now she is at home to rest, and it makes her worse. I don't think she likes it. She gets so angry. And she is as mean to her child. Oh, she pounces down on everybody." Then after a pause, and in a low voice, "I wish, gosh, I wish just my mother and I would live together. I never said anything like this to anybody, but that's what I wish."

ELAINE said this almost fearfully, almost as if she would hurt her sister by saying it. W said this wish was very natural because her sister was the one who was disturbing them. It was very possible that her sister also wished she were by herself, and maybe someday this could be worked out. W then said that things might be better when ELAINE goes to school, because then she will not be at home all day. ELAINE agreed that that would make a lot of difference, since she would come home only in the evening. She said that her sister even yells at her mother, but her mother usually takes ELAINE's part. W got the impression that ELAINE was identifying herself very strongly with her mother, and not only wanted protection from her mother, but also wanted to protect her mother herself.

At about this point VIRGINIA arrived, and ELAINE stopped talking about her problems. VIRGINIA looked very pretty and was nicely dressed for the visit to the planetarium. She said right away that she had told W last time that she'd like to have a library card, and now she wondered whether W would go with her and get one before we went to the planetarium. She asked rather hesitantly whether she would be allowed to take out books right away. W said she was sure she could. The whole process of getting the library card was a gratifying experience for VIRGINIA. When we came to the desk the librarian said first that VIRGINIA would need identification, and VIRGINIA looked very disappointed. Then she remembered that she had a letter in her pocket, which proved to be all she needed. She was radiant with joy when she learned that she could get her library card today.

It happened that a librarian W knew was in the library, so W introduced VIRGINIA to her. This was a great help, since the librarian knew the place well and could show VIRGINIA how to find books. VIRGINIA wanted a special book about a young girl. The librarian could not find that one, but introduced VIRGINIA to another book, and showed her different kinds of books she would enjoy. VIRGINIA was quite surprised to find that she could take out ten books at a time. She chose three books, apparently very good ones concerning young girls, one about a young Negro girl. When W asked her whether she should help her carry the books, VIRGINIA smiled and said, "I love to carry books." Then she added, "You know, I feel swell. I just feel grown-up." It meant a great deal to her.

VIRGINIA had asked ELAINE whether she also wanted to come to the library, but ELAINE had stayed outside looking at a book with pictures of art that W had brought with her. While W and VIRGINIA walked back to join ELAINE, W told her that ELAINE was quite unhappy and had wanted to talk about it, and that she might want to continue. VIRGINIA said thoughtfully, "I know, it's just like I was." Outside, the three of us waited for EILEEN for quite a long time, but when she did not come we decided to walk a short way into the park, rest there until one o'clock, eat our lunch, and then go to the planetarium.

On the way VIRGINIA started talking about her uncle. She said that he was getting married, and that she would like to go to the wedding and get a new formal. W smiled and asked how often she had worn her old formal. She said five times, and it seemed too often. She then talked in a very friendly way about this uncle, with whom she apparently had a good relationship.

ELAINE walked along quietly; then, suddenly, as if coming out of deep thought, she said, "You know, I just thought about my sister. I think she can just jump in the lake." W smiled and said it might be a good idea to think about it that way, and not to care too much what her sister said about her. ELAINE said, "I don't know whether I used the right expression, but I think it's necessary that I don't care so terribly much about her." VIRGINIA said that was just it, and you don't have to think of what other people think of you. We talked a little more about this, emphasizing the fact that we are what we are, whether or not people look down on us, or call us dumb, or whatever they do. This meant something both to ELAINE and to VIRGINIA. Both girls said they had sometimes been looked down upon, but maybe it was important just to feel that you are not bad, and that way you could get along.

As we sat down on the grass ELAINE said, "Really, I shouldn't complain so much." VIRGINIA quickly said, "Oh, yes, you should. It's much better to talk about it. We're all not always happy, and I was very unhappy once." She then told ELAINE, as she had told THELMA before, about her own unhappiness and the conflict between her father and mother. Again, she told it in the past tense, as if she was much happier now. She added this time that her father wasn't very good yet, but that she got along very well with her mother. She said that they went out a lot together and things were going so much better, and that it helped a lot just to talk about it. ELAINE said that it had been worse since the death of her father. When her father died, her sister became so ugly to her. Before that, her sister would never have dared to act like that. It's interesting that ELAINE ties up her sister's behavior with her father's death. She said she felt a longing every time she saw a streetcar marked "C." [the neighborhood she formerly lived in]. That had been the happiest time. She also talked about the fact that their house was just too crowded. They got on each other's nerves, and that way her sister started yelling and being unhappy.

W asked when her sister had been doing these things, and ELAINE mentioned an incident of the previous evening. ELAINE's sister had gone out and had asked ELAINE to turn on the stove to heat some water. It got quite late and ELAINE forgot to turn on the gas stove. ELAINE said, "I really don't forget so many things, but I do forget some. It isn't so bad, she could put it on herself, couldn't she?" Then she continued, "Well, I had forgotten it, and it was so late I had gone to bed already and started to sleep. When she came home and found the water wasn't hot, she made a terrible scene and screamed why hadn't I done it. She wakes everybody up. Mother was on my side but it doesn't help too much." Then, looking at Virginia, she asked, "Do you have any brothers or sisters?" Virginia said she had none. [This was the first time that Virginia did not mention her little boy as her brother.] But she added that she had a lot of cousins who were always staying at the house, and that wasn't so easy either. She was so often compared to them, and because she was taller, she always had to give in. Then she added, "Maybe it's sometimes good to fight back," and Elaine nodded.

The conversation became a little more relaxed and the girls took out their lunches. Elaine said at first that she wasn't hungry, but soon she started eating. Virginia asked the others to eat one of her egg sandwiches. She was very proud because she had fixed the eggs herself, and she gave the recipe to W. She also gave W one of the cookies she had baked. She was really proud of her achievement in cooking. Elaine said that she liked cooking too. The talk then drifted to the subject of history, and when Elaine suddenly found out that Virginia liked history too, she was quite surprised. She said, "Well, you like just the same things as I do; I never knew that." Elaine said this in a surprised and happy tone of voice, and Virginia looked pleased. W felt that it meant a lot to both of them, not only because each had found another girl who had the same interests, but also because a white and a colored girl had found that they had the same interests and wishes.

While they were eating, W told the girls that just that morning she had got some letters from friends in Germany. One of them told about the school situation there, and W read a little about it. W had also received that same day a letter from a fifteen-year-old girl in France, and W read this to them too. They both enjoyed listening, and talked about how terrible it was that people had suffered so much over there. ELAINE said that she had relatives in Germany, and added, "They were people who were against the Nazis." It seemed to mean a lot to ELAINE that she could identify herself with the people who had written these letters to W. They talked about how bad it was that there was racial discrimination here and in Germany, and W said it was sad that people looked down upon others. They had seen that when they talked about their own personal problems, and the same thing was happening in nations too. Both girls nodded, and VIRGINIA said that discrimination was so unnecessary.

ELAINE seemed to feel much calmer now than in the beginning, and the girls started talking about other things and the coming trip to the planetarium. VIRGINIA had been there once, but ELAINE had never been there and was excited about it. When VIRGINIA mentioned that it was dark in the planetarium, ELAINE asked twice, rather anxiously, whether it was spooky. Both VIRGINIA and W told her that it wasn't—that it was just dark and nothing to be afraid of. On the way down in the streetcar ELAINE asked the names of different places they were passing, but VIRGINIA read some of the magazines W had brought along. At the planetarium they first walked through the building, looking at the different displays. ELAINE was very intent on it all and read many of the descriptions with great interest. Often W did not understand the exhibits and said so, but they enjoyed the parts which they understood. There was an exhibit of electrical work that showed the men at work. ELAINE said, "My father was an electrician." When W said that was highly skilled work, she looked pleased and then said, "Say that again, what you said." W repeated it, and ELAINE smiled again, very pleased.

We got very tired from all this looking, so after going to a drugstore for a drink, we entered the sky show. ELAINE was like a child led into fairyland. W has seldom seen anyone so happy there. Even in the beginning, she couldn't get over the beautiful soft music, which she recognized as classical music. She enjoyed the soft gleam and the pictures around

her. She whispered that she didn't feel it was spooky at all—
it was just beautiful.

The sky show was an interesting one and both girls listened
intently. At one point, when the lecturer talked about how
maybe someday the world would end, VIRGINIA shivered, said
it was cold in the room, and snuggled up to W. W put her
arm around her, and she stayed very close to W. When the
stars came out ELAINE said, "Oh, how beautiful! I wish my
mother could see this." Every time ELAINE sees something
that impresses her especially, she adds that she wishes her
mother could see it.

After the sky show both girls had to look at the machine.
ELAINE said she thought it was just wonderful the way the
lecturer had spoken. He had explained so simply scientific
facts that otherwise seemed so complicated. She said it was so
beautiful that she would have to go there again, and added,
"This city has wonderful things. I always thought I was a
country girl, but now I think I like the city too." She added
that she had been with her mother to see the museum, after
the group had visited there, and that she very much wanted
to bring her mother to see this too. She also said, "This was
the most beautiful thing I have ever seen in my life." VIR-
GINIA seemed impressed too, but was not as outspoken as
ELAINE because it wasn't completely new to her.

We all took the streetcar into town together and then
separated. ELAINE and W took one car, while VIRGINIA took
another. The girls waved to each other as if they had become
real friends. On the way home ELAINE said smilingly that she
thought VIRGINIA had been a little afraid when there was so
much noise and the lecturer had talked about the end of the
world. When W said that VIRGINIA might have been, ELAINE
said she could understand that, but it was so beautiful that
she forgot to be afraid. She said she would go right back to
see her mother, because she had to tell her about it. She added,
"I sure forgot all about the trouble with my sister."

Fourteenth Meeting

A trip to the zoo had been planned for this meeting. ELAINE, as usual, was the first one to arrive. The psychologist had asked W to give ELAINE the results of the test she had taken with the intention of entering school. W explained the results to ELAINE, and the fact that they were good made her extremely happy. She was amazed that in so many places she had been able to score a higher grade than when she left school. W told her that keeping up with her reading probably had had a lot to do with it. She was riding on a cloud all day because of the test results, and every so often while walking she would return to the subject. In a rather shy way she asked W if she would give her a copy of the results so she could show them to her mother. W said that this usually wasn't done, but that W wouldn't mind giving them to her if she would bring them back. She said she'd just love to show them to her mother.

When VIRGINIA arrived she was very much interested in the test results too, and said she might make similar grades, at least as far as the low arithmetic score was concerned. The two girls wanted to go into the library, and they asked W a little hesitantly whether she would mind if they went inside. W said she didn't mind at all and would wait outside to see whether THELMA would come. They stayed quite a little while in the library. Later, on the way to the streetcar, we met THELMA.

The visit to the zoo was enjoyable in every way. The girls liked being able to look around leisurely and to choose whatever they wanted to see. While they were feeding the deer, ELAINE said she liked the deer best of all the animals. At one point, the father deer kept pushing away the young deer and prevented the girls from giving food to the youngest one. THELMA said, "I should tell my father that today I met somebody who is just like he is."

THELMA very often hung behind the others and stood a long time at cages they had passed. Usually, however, she caught up with us again after a while. We finally sat down in the warm sunshine. THELMA and VIRGINIA wanted to learn how to crochet, and W showed them. THELMA became very impatient and didn't show too much skill, but VIRGINIA caught on quickly. After a while THELMA said that W had given VIRGINIA the better yarn, so it was easier for her. VIRGINIA immediately offered to exchange, so she took the yarn that THELMA had used and THELMA took VIRGINIA's. ELAINE said she was too tired. She pulled out her test results, and thoroughly enjoyed looking at them over and over again. VIRGINIA suddenly put her head down and said she had terrible pains in her neck from doing a lot of house cleaning the day before. Both VIRGINIA and THELMA lay down on the grass, and ELAINE asked if she couldn't go out and explore a little. W said she certainly could, but she walked only a few steps and then said she was afraid of getting lost. W asked VIRGINIA and THELMA whether it would be all right for W to go along with ELAINE for a little while, saying that they wouldn't go too far.

At first ELAINE was quite anxious and said she was afraid to leave the two girls alone; but when W said they were old enough and would not always be under supervision, she came along. ELAINE and W walked a little while and finally came to the water reservoir in the park. ELAINE exclaimed over its beauty. She talked about how glad she was that she was going back to school now, and how she was sure that things would come out all right.

When ELAINE and W rejoined the other girls they asked whether they could do something special next time. VIRGINIA said she would like to invite some of her friends, and THELMA said she would too. ELAINE said she had no friends. When the other two just couldn't understand how it happened that ELAINE had no friends, she said in a loud voice, "Well, I can't help it. I didn't go to school for three years. This darn St. Vitus' dance, I told you about it." The two girls nodded and said that usually you don't have friends if you aren't in school, but that after ELAINE had been in school she would have many more. VIRGINIA said she could bring both boys and

girls. THELMA said she would try to bring some girls, but she
was sure she wouldn't bring any boys.

While they were lying there in the grass, VIRGINIA sometimes looked sad and the girls asked her what was the matter.
Each time she shook her head and said nothing. Finally
ELAINE, with a twinkle in her eye, looked at VIRGINIA gravely
and said, "I think I know what it is, VIRGINIA—you're in love."
The girls all laughed, and THELMA said, "She's almost as good
as the psychiatrist." That seemed to please ELAINE a lot, and
she laughed and said, "Well, VIRGINIA, you certainly have
that look in your eyes." VIRGINIA nodded her head and said
it was true, and then they agreed that it must be Bobbie, who
had left for the army.

There was a lot of talk about what it was like being in love.
THELMA said that soon ELAINE would be in love too, and
they laughed about it and kidded each other. Once THELMA
said it was surprising how many friends VIRGINIA had, but
VIRGINIA said they were just friends and she was not in love
with them. W said that boys and girls could work and play
together without always being in love. ELAINE said yes, that
was the way it had been with the boys in C. She hoped it
could be that way again, and later she would fall in love with
one or another. THELMA said it was much better to know lots
of boys and not just fall for one.

It was time to walk back. The girls walked arm in arm,
VIRGINIA making fun and imitating different movie actresses.
ELAINE too joined in the fun completely. Once THELMA said
that W's arms felt so wonderful, and that she wished she had
a soft arm. W said that THELMA's arms were good and strong.
THELMA said, "Do you think they are dependable arms? I
was told that was good in marriage."

PROGRESS REPORTS ON THREE OF THE GIRLS

Thelma

Thelma was referred to the clinic by her mother because of strange physical symptoms—crying, grinning, and enuresis. Thelma was in conflict with her mother. She could understand her mother in many ways—she talked about her mother's hard childhood, and how little interest her father took in bringing up the children—yet she resented her mother's too high and too strict standards, and her refusal to let the girls have sufficient recreational outlets.

Thelma made excellent use of the group. She was free and outspoken in discussing her problems, which were mainly the conflict with her parents and sibling rivalry. There was also a rejection of herself. She said once, "Nobody really loves me." She thought of herself as unattractive, too heavy, slow-moving, and "dumb." She had high standards of living, and her ambition was to become a singer and go to college. She wanted to have things done nicely. Her food was always neatly packed—she did this herself—and she said that she liked food prepared and served so that it was pleasing to the eye. Thelma showed many fears, mostly connected with sex—fear of menstrual pain, of pain in childbirth, and of woods and snakes.

It helped Thelma a great deal to have a place where she could talk about her problems and where she was thoroughly accepted. This acceptance by W and the other girls was a main factor in helping Thelma to make a more happy adjustment. She learned that she was not the only one who had conflicts at home. The girls liked her and gave her approval when she came to meetings with a new dress or hair-do. Her positive physical features were stressed until Thelma learned that she was not ugly. The change in her appearance that came with increasing self-confidence was amazing, and she actually became pretty.

128

Intensive case work with Thelma's mother helped her to recognize Thelma's recreational needs and need for independence. In February she allowed Thelma to take singing lessons and to join the YWCA. Certainly not all of the conflicts were solved, but Thelma herself summarized the situation by saying, "Mother sure has changed. She lets me go out more; she trusts me more. Well, sometimes it is not so good and father gets mad; but those things I can work through by myself." Thelma's physical symptoms, including the enuresis, had disappeared, and she hoped to go to camp the following summer.

Virginia

When Virginia was first seen she was a rather unhappy-looking girl, almost sullen; but she quickly responded to acceptance by W and the other girls. She soon became lively and outgoing, and showed warm, helpful attitudes toward her contemporaries. She talked during the first meetings about her conflicts at home—how hard it was not to be allowed to go out, and her dissatisfaction with her father. She also mentioned that it was hard on her to be so tall because people expected her to act older than she was. She was happy in active group games, and showed interest in sports, sewing, and cooking. From the first she was positive toward school. After camp she experienced a very happy period. She had loved camp.

In the clinic's day camp she was able to help the other girls feel comfortable and wanted. She was especially close to her mother during these months, and spoke with much appreciation of her mother's understanding, and how they helped each other. She got interested in reading good books, and when she took out a library card she said with satisfaction, "Now I feel almost grown-up." She had from the beginning a healthy attitude toward boys. She would talk of boy friends with interest, but matter-of-factly. Virginia brought three boys and two girls as guests to a wiener roast. Her behavior in the presence of the boys was that of a friendly companion, with some rough and tumble play.

Virginia's happy development was interrupted by the arrest of her father. She feared being ostracized by her contemporaries and feared the gossip of neighbors. She felt the family's financial stress, and also suffered from her mother's tenseness. She saw her father in court on the day of the trial and started to idealize him. Soon afterward she became irregular in group attendance. Sometimes she stayed away because her mother had become ill, and Virginia had to shoulder a great deal of responsibility. She carried many household duties after school and had little chance to go out. Her attitude toward this situation was a mixture of unusual maturity and adolescent impatience. In individual contacts she expressed her understanding of the necessity for her doing this work, and of her mother's "crabbiness," as she called it, but she felt too much cooped up.

The moment her mother felt better, Virginia thought she should have more freedom. The conflict between Virginia and her mother sharpened. Virginia told about receiving a severe beating with a telephone cord, when she had come home late one night. She was especially humiliated and resentful because the marks could be seen on her arms and legs. At this time she also talked about some difficulty in school, because she talked too much; but she expressed her definite intention to go through school and make good. She reported three months later that things were going better in school. At this time it seemed that Virginia was ready to join a neighborhood group, and that the group at the clinic had fulfilled its purpose.

Elaine

In every one of these meetings Elaine showed definite progress, largely because she was always aware of the purpose of her coming to the clinic and had a great desire to overcome her sickness.

When Elaine entered the group she was extremely shy and withdrawn. She looked very pretty with her hair hanging down, and wore a pale blue dress and a bunch of violets on her shoulder. This showed interest in her appearance, but she looked much younger than her age. After long moments of silence during the first meeting, the girls finally started talking about their interests. Elaine then felt free to mention her interest in ancient history, music, painting, and trips. It was then, apparently, that she felt for the first time the acceptance of contemporaries. She looked apologetic when she talked about her interest in ancient history, but was very relieved when nobody sneered. At this first meeting the girls discovered volleyball and had a game outside. Elaine ran for the ball, jumped, and caught it well. At the end of the meeting she said, "This was the first time in three years that I played ball and I like it." This ball game was the beginning of a loosening-up process, physically and emotionally. It gave Elaine great satisfaction to know that she could run and play like anybody else, and later she expressed several times her amazement at not getting tired.

She was anxious to overcome her slowness and awkwardness. At the third meeting the group had a birthday party for one of the girls, and Elaine smiled happily when she was asked to light the candles. She got quite impatient with herself when she didn't succeed right away and said, "I'm too slow for this, maybe somebody else can do it." But the friendliness of the girls helped her to continue.

In the fourth meeting Elaine was alone for a while with W and one of the other girls. The other girl asked Elaine why she hadn't been in school for such a long time. Elaine told the story of her sickness with a tortured facial expression, but she was determined to go through with it. She expressed her unhappiness about not having understood her sickness, but also her relief that it was getting better. It apparently meant a great deal to her that a girl of her own age did not laugh at her. During this time Elaine was especially reluctant to enter any conversation regarding boys. When the girls asked her about a boy friend, she said she didn't know much about boys. "I'm just a country girl." It was also at this time that she told her mother of her dislike for one of the "boy crazy" girls.

There was a definite change around the sixth and seventh meetings. At this time the group was going on several trips. Elaine was not only impressed with all the new things she saw, but came in closer contact with the other girls. She missed the girl she had disliked at first, saying, "It does me good to have our Laughing Bird around. I have to learn to laugh too." She talked more freely with the girls and carried the coat of a colored girl over her arm, although she had objected to touching these clothes before.

The day camp program during the summer increased her security with others She talked freely about her German background, about her relatives, and her longing for the countryside, but after a few trips she was able to say, "I start liking the city when I find out what it has to offer." She expressed her resentment toward her sister, describing how she could not sleep because of their quarrels; but after some discussion with the others, she suddenly said, "I think she can just jump in the lake." This was a most unusual expression coming from Elaine, and showed her increased assimilation to the language of her own generation.

During the summer Elaine took some achievement tests in preparation for her entrance into school. She was very anxious about them, and her comparatively good results on them bolstered her self-confidence a great deal. Her native sense of humor came out, and she was able to tease one of the girls about being in love, saying, "You have that look in your eyes."

After her successful entrance into high school Elaine was overjoyed with the school experience. She arrived at her first group meeting in the fall with a new permanent, a new dress, and a string of beads around her neck. She was ambitious in school, and it meant a lot to her that she made the honor roll. At the same time, she was very aware of her increasingly good social adjustment. She talked now about having friends among the girls—"The boys are much too young," she said—

going out with them and talking to them. She told about an incident when somebody had pulled a chair from under her, and she had said, "If you do that again I'll punch you in the nose." The applause she got from the clinic group showed her how well she was becoming a part of the club.

Elaine still avoided parties, however, even at the clinic. The Christmas party was the first she came to. At this party she and another girl from the clinic group sang for the whole company, including adults. She had been afraid of this and told W later that she had trembled all over; but she was very happy that she had done it and she really had enjoyed it. She started participating in the school choir, and said she had overcome her fear of standing there on the stage.

In the last group meeting she expressed several times her concern about "acting younger than her age." This seemed to be a good sign in the maturing process. For the first time Elaine began seeking information on how to use make-up. When W mentioned the difference between make-up for daytime and for a date, Elaine looked up, rather surprised, and said, "I really should meet some older boys." During the summer W had brought the magazine Seventeen to the group. In spite of the enthusiasm of the other girls for it, Elaine had hardly looked at it. Now she asked whether she could take it home. When she brought it back she said she thought it was wonderful, and that she didn't know why she hadn't read it before. She pointed out a story about a young girl who had been very much afraid of her first party, and quite apparently identified herself with this girl.

In January W contacted a settlement house and asked whether there would be activities for Elaine. The house had several different activities to offer, among them piano lessons, which Elaine wanted very much to take. She was getting so much satisfaction out of the school experience too that she planned to continue another year, and to work during the summer if that was possible. She summarized her own development by saying, "I wonder sometimes why I did not want to meet people. I hardly understand it now."

POSTSCRIPT

These records are presented for the analysis and study of a method. There is nothing dramatic about the group work method. Help in release and control of feelings, in adjustment to oneself and to others, in understanding values, in learning to give and accept trust, and in making one's own decisions and carrying them out—such help takes effect slowly, in small doses, more through day-to-day living than through much verbal expression. Accepting the job of a police officer in a boys' game and learning that it does not give one the right to punish anybody; choosing the color of a bead, as Elaine did after three years of not daring to make a decision; learning that an adult will let you butter a bun even if you do not always wash your neck well—all these achievements do seem rather unimportant. Yet added together they can rightly be called therapeutic, for they help to unravel and overcome all the snarls and distrusts and inadequacies that have developed in an unhappy youngster. It is the group worker's art to observe all these small events and to make constructive use of them.

"For the great things are not done by impulse, but by a series of small things brought together."

VINCENT VAN GOGH in a letter
to his brother Theo